Janice Day grew up in Berkshire and now lives with her two children and her cat Rolo in Epsom in Surrey. After ⟨...⟩ ...mingham University in the late 1970s, she worked part-time as a secretarial temp and sang for the Piccadilly Dance Orchestra and Cotton Club Orchestra at weekends.

In 1996 she was diagnosed with breast cancer. Given a fifty percent chance of survival by her doctors, she determined to pursue her lifelong ambition to become a writer. *Getting It Off My Chest* is her first book.

www.janiceday.wordpress.com

How I Lost My Breast & found Myself

GETTING IT OFF My Chest

Janice Day

Old St PUBLISHING

First published in 2009 by Old Street Publishing Ltd
40 Bowling Green Lane, London EC1R 0NE
www.oldstreetpublishing.co.uk

ISBN 978-1-905847-89-1
Copyright © Janice Day 2009

10 9 8 7 6 5 4 3 2 1

A CIP catalogue record for this title is available from the
British Library.

Printed and bound in Great Britain.

To Joy Norman, who set me the task of writing this book

'I Fear Thee, Ancient Mariner!'

The night before my operation, the very old lady in the next bed suddenly accosted me.

She held me with her skinny hand and told me I would reinvent myself and like what I became.

Looking back down the years between then and now I can see that she was right.

I did reinvent myself and I really do like what I became.

And you don't have to have breast cancer, by the way, to do that.

1963 My Mother's Teeth

The very first debt I owed was the price in pain of my mother's teeth. After all, it was my fault that she broke one on a toffee and ran down the road to the dentist to have thirteen of them removed at once.

For it was I who 'stole her calcium' as I lay plotting in her belly. I often wondered how I came to be such a fiend. What ancient secret of calcium-extraction had I learned and instantly forgotten in my journey from embryo to foetus?

Then I compounded the felony by not only being a fortnight overdue but by thoughtlessly protracting the labour pains for two whole days and splitting my poor old Mum from 'ere to 'ere' when I finally came out. I looked carefully for the scars of this grievous bodily harm, carefully and often, not being entirely sure where 'ere to 'ere' might be. Perhaps it was beneath my mother's heavily corseted torso. Or maybe God took the scars away, in compensation for the loss of her teeth.

I was very young when she told me all this. I sat, transfixed, on the old tin boiler, wilfully inviting the onset of piles and chilblains. But I didn't mind. My bum was pleasantly warm and I sat, eyes fixed on my mother's face, as I swung my olive-green-clad legs up in the air and listened with horror to the story of my birth.

'And when you finally came out,' she whispered, as if it were truly a ghoulish tale, 'all your skin was peeling off and you had little breasts oozing milk.'

'But why?!' I cried, in horror.

'Because you stayed so long. You carried on growing up and shed your first set of skin. And then you started turning into a woman, ahead of your time.'

Thus it was that I slunk into the world from the primordial ooze, where creatures of my ilk hang out.

And kindly Mum, even though I had cost her the thirteen original teeth with lashings of terrible pain and suffering, kindly old Mum was generous enough to offer up her false teeth as a cabaret act to my school friends.

'Do that thing with your teeth, Mum,' I'd clamour. And after some becoming reluctance, she would eventually be persuaded to dislodge her top gnashers with her tongue and expose for one instant her shiny pink gums to the assembled company, which caused us all to shriek and run away.

'What's for tea?' we'd sneak back and ask.

'Bread and dripping,' she would say, although it never was, not ever.

22 August 1996
'Have you had a nice summer?'

'Knickers,' said Mr Sausages, and twenty-six children screamed with laughter. It was my son Michael's fifth birthday party, in a sunny, dusty church hall, somewhere in Surrey. I was putting party food into the jungle-themed cardboard boxes and pouring blackcurrant and orange juice into paper cups. I did it methodically. It was comforting.

My friend Penny came over, looking happy. I tensed.

'How are you? How's Mark? Have you had a nice summer?' she said.

I looked up, not wanting to, and had a strange experience. Penny seemed to be looking at me from across a great divide. She stood on the far side of a ravine, in the land where people have nice summers and look forward to sending their children back to school. And I stood in the shadow land, where people have cancer. The hall darkened and shrank until there were only the two of us. Dark water swirled around my feet.

'Janice?'

'What?'

My stomach clenched. I moved the cups into a straight line on the counter, orange followed by blackcurrant followed by orange. I looked at my handiwork. It was no good. The distance between each cup was erratic. Carefully, I moved them all along again until the line was perfect.

'What are you doing?' she laughed.

I looked at her again. The hall was back to normal. It was hot and I was aware that some of the mums were watching us. Mr Sausage's amplifying system was blaring out toilet jokes and the children were giggling and rolling about on the dusty floor. Penny and I were alone at the bar and the nearest person was twenty feet away, but I was still afraid that my secret might be overheard.

I didn't want to say it; didn't want to change her world; didn't want her to catch it too. But it had to come out sooner or later.

'They think I might have breast cancer,' I said.

I watched her reaction. She gasped and gripped my forearm.

'You must let me help you,' she said. I looked at the hand on my arm and then up at her face. How could she help me? Could she make it better? I was drowning and there was no one in the pool but me. Then I remembered.

'You're a nurse,' I said. 'Of course you are…' She nodded, accepting without question that I had forgotten something so familiar: she worked as a recovery nurse in a cancer centre. Silly me. But since the previous day's diagnosis, everything was being relearned: pouring juice into cups, a child's laugh, a friend's history. All were bright, crisp, new experiences, brought to me one by one to examine while I whirled helplessly in the dark water.

1991 Becoming Breast-Aware

26 November 1991

Dear Dr E

Thank you for seeing this lady who had a baby in August of this year and has a persistent one cm breast lump lateral to the left nipple.

She is still breast-feeding and I would be grateful for your opinion.

Yours sincerely

Dr A

7 January 1992

Dear Dr A

Thank you for referring this 34-year-old lady with a lump in her left breast. She is at present breast-feeding her 4-month-old baby and it is during this time that she has noticed the lump. Her menarche was at 11; she has had operations for tonsillectomy and adenoidectomy. There is no previous history of breast disease and no family history of breast cancer.

On examination there is a hard, mobile, round lump at 4 o'clock on the left breast. Ultrasound of the lump proved this to be a cystic lesion. We do not need to take any action at present and I have asked her to continue lactation as planned and to come for review when she stops, and we will probably then discharge her back to your care.

Yours sincerely

Dr E

Senior Registrar – Medical Breast Unit

I began to examine my breasts once a month, getting to know their lumps and bumps, so four years later it was easy for me to notice something out of the ordinary.

'Doctor, Doctor, everyone says I'm invisible...' 'Who said that?'

How innocently I had skipped into the doctor's surgery sixteen days before Michael's party. Just another Surrey Housewife. A fully paid-up member of the Great Worried Well.

'Actually, it's not just one lump,' I quipped merrily. 'It's more like a family of four have moved in with suitcases.'

I could joke because I wasn't worried, having had a breast lump before, when Michael was six weeks old. The doctor had packed me off to the local cancer centre, where they informed me that it was a milk cyst and nothing to worry about.

Nine out of ten lumps, I was told, turn out to be benign. That first lump was definitely benign. In fact it saved my life: it made me 'breast-aware'. And being breast-aware, I examined myself with the flat of my hand once a month, although I was not afraid of what I might find, since I was living proof of the kindliness of lumps.

My breast and I were friends. I knew all its lumps and bumps. So when I came across this one, I thought it would be the same story: that it would be benign, especially as it wasn't the pea-sized lump of cancer legend, but more like a thickening of the skin.

I was pretty low at the time. An incurable hypochondriac, I was almost never genuinely ill, but the winter before they discovered the cancer in my breast I caught one virus after another. I kept going back to the doctor, complaining that I was feeling tired and stressed. And I *was* massively tired; a tiredness that settled in my bones and didn't go away.

I suppose the feeling of exhaustion could have been my immune system breaking down – overloaded as it was with sugar, fat and stress – so that it was no match for the rogue cancer cell that one day ran out of control.

On the other hand, it could have been the fact that I didn't get enough sleep and lived at the top of a hill.

Or it could have been, as the doctor suggested, something to do with my two small children. 'Show me a mother of two small children who isn't tired,' he said.

Now I was back at the surgery again, with a mole, a lump and a bony ankle. I was more worried about the extra bone growing in my ankle than the lump in my breast. I had seen a disturbing sight once in Marks & Spencer: a man with an extraordinarily large head, his skull having burgeoned spectacularly in an apparent effort to turn him into Frankenstein's monster. Of course I was convinced the same thing would happen to me. Why wouldn't it? Wasn't I already born a monster with peeling skin and little breasts oozing milk? Giant skull disease was only a matter of time...

'Shall we start at the bottom and work our way up?' said the doctor. 'Let's do the extra bone in your ankle, the mole on your arm and the lump in your breast, in that order.'

I nodded, took off my bra and watched sadly as my breasts plummeted towards Australia, summarily dismissing the mole on my upper arm to the back of the queue.

But the doctor was polite and followed the original plan. The protuberance on my anklebone was caused by a recent sprain, where the ligament had torn away a fragment of bone and the bone had grown back more thickly to compensate. I wasn't turning into a mutant after all. The arm thing was just a thing: unidentifiable and uninteresting.

And the breast lump? Oh, that. I was determined not to think very much about that. He asked me to lie down while he examined me.

I was about seven stone heavier than I am now and had a big fat tummy. It was the sort of tummy that my small daughter could bury her toys in when we were in the bath and watch them slowly reappear. I didn't exactly feel like a sex goddess, so to overcome my embarrassment at being examined by my deliciously gorgeous doctor I floated off into a romantic fantasy about him.

'Ah, Carissima,' he said. 'Where have you been? It's been so long since I saw you...'

'But, Brett,' she said, because his name really ought to be Brett, 'it was only last week. Don't you remember my little bout of rabies?'

'You are so-o-o beautiful... Please let me lie beside you. Say I can?'

Deftly, he leapt up onto the bed – which had miraculously gained a foot in width – and planted little butterfly kisses all over her body while at the same time caressing her everywhere with his huge hands. Despite his untamed brutishness, he was gentle; as gentle as a... um... a doctor.

When my brain reconnected to my body I noticed that the examination was over. I was getting dressed again and was alarmed to find myself speaking.

I've learned from bitter experience that it's not a good idea to speak when your brain is busy elsewhere. When I tuned into my mouth I found it asking him the difference between a pessary and a suppository. Not the best chat-up line.

He answered politely. 'Well, the first goes up your vagina and the second goes up your bottom.'

I could think of no way to retrieve the situation so I just nodded wisely. He looked at me for a while and then spoke.

'There's definitely a lump there,' he said. 'Shall we wait a month and see what happens?'

'No.'

The voice was firm and assertive. It was not flirtatious,

silly, breathy or girlish. In fact it was none of my usual voices. Where did it come from? We were both impressed.

'No. Of course. We shouldn't wait at all,' he said and with a single, panther-like bound... well, anyway, he picked up the phone, rang the hospital and made absolutely sure that I would be seen for a mammogram on Friday, which was just three days away.

My Ordinary Life

15 August 1996

Dear Lou,

I am appalled that I haven't written for so long. It's a disgrace! Especially when I wanted to say hearty congratulations for being up the duff, in the club, rotund, fecund, moribund and burgeoning. Well done!

My own news is long and tedious. I sprained my ankle in March. The man across the street told me to sue the council and that's what I'm doing.

I also recently found a lump in my breast and went for a mammogram. I'm warning you now never, ever to submit yourself to this really horrible experience. I was pushed and pulled and contorted into unbelievable positions by two beefy women who all the while muttered obscurely about the apparently very strange bosoms before them, saying things like, 'Hmmm, it really is a very long attachment isn't it?'

What on earth is that supposed to mean? And is it bad?

When they finally managed to get the offending glands onto the pathetically small platform, they lowered the top paddle-thingy and squeezed my tits until I thought I was going to come out of there with two pepperoni pizzas attached to my sternum.

They then decided that it all had to be done again because they could see from the first pictures that I had a lump in my breast – which I already knew – and they wanted a magnification.

At the end of it I said, 'I don't wish to appear ungrateful but I can tell you now that even if my breasts suddenly appear to be hanging by a thread or swell to the size of beach balls, I am never going to go through that again.' They laughed.

I asked them if I had a particularly deformed chest, to see if that was the problem, and they cheerily told me that it was the same performance with everyone. Call me a cynic, but I can't help thinking that if men had breasts the equipment used for mammograms would miraculously improve…

Anyway, I'm summoned to the breast clinic. The doctor assures me that it's probably just a 'cyst' that'll need 'draining'. Another delightful experience I'm sure.

Maybe I should try and think of a better hobby than hypochondria. I'll bet that all the doctors and nurses in the county of Surrey are putting their heads together and plotting how to get rid of Janice Day, once and for all.

Mmmmm, yes, paranoia. Now, that's a good hobby…

Write soon!

Jx

A Density

There was a moment there with the jolly, beefy ladies when everything stopped: laughter, time, my heart.

It was such a tiny change in behaviour, as they hunched together over the mammograms. The cheerfulness became less genuine. The eyes roved a little from mine. But it was chillingly clear to me that the light-heartedness of moments ago had flitted delicately out of the room.

I asked them if they could see anything and they said, 'Well, there is a density there.' A density? They wouldn't explain, saying that the radiologist would look at it and probably call me in to the breast clinic. Just routine, they said.

Just routine? Isn't that what a policeman says to the prime suspect?

They pointed to the picture, proud of their expertise, and sober too, because they knew – or seemed to know – that they might be holding my ticket to cross the Styx.

One of the ladies indicated a little white star; a blank centre from which some white lines fanned. And then others. Smaller ones.

They were so pretty.

The Result

DEPARTMENT OF CLINICAL RADIOLOGY
Exam date: 09.08.96
Examinations Requested:
L MAMMOGRAM
R MAMMOGRAM

Clinical information: Increased nodularity lateral left breast. Discrete nodule lateral to nipple.

Full Result: MAMMOGRAMS: The left breast shows abnormal appearances over a wide area. There are multiple spiculating stellate lesions, mostly in the superior lateral quadrant, but also extending toward the central area of the breast. There is distortion of the upper outer margin of the glandular tissue. There is associated microcalcification. There are at least three stellate areas and there is one rounded opacity, less than 1cm in diameter, which is also associated with microcalcification. There is a smooth nodular opacity higher up towards the axilla, which could be a fibroadenoma or a lymph node.

The right breast is relatively normal mammographically, but does show a faint streaky opacity in the upper outer quadrant which is regarded with some suspicion in view of the findings in the left breast.

COMMENT: Reference to Breast Clinic is advised (GP has been telephoned).

Dr B, Consultant Radiologist

12 August 1996

Dear Mr C

Thank you for seeing this lady urgently in your Breast Clinic, as advised by Doctor B who telephoned me yesterday with a verbal report of a highly suspicious mammogram.

Janice presented to me on the 6th August, with a tender lump in the left breast which had been present for two weeks. On examination there was a palpable nodule in the left breast with other multiple nodules. I could detect no abnormal lymph nodes and no other abnormality.

Past medical history includes two normal pregnancies and healthy children, 1994 gastroscopy showing hiatus hernia and H pylori positive.

She is a singer, she is married. The family history is only of ischaemic heart disease and late onset diabetes.

Many thanks for your early advice.

Yours sincerely

Dr A

She is a Singer. She is Married.

15 August 1996

Dear Josie,

I've just written a great long letter to Lou and it's made me feel so guilty about neglecting you that I must now write another to you and I've already run out of interesting things to say so here is a page of drivel! It's your own fault for moving to Milan.

So. Enough about you. Let me tell you about my latest Grand Master Plan.

Mark wants to move out of this area to somewhere like Shropshire. One of his brilliant ideas.

I've resisted this because it would mean that I would find it hard to get singing work. On the other hand, that might be a good thing. I mean, I keep saying that I'm going to give up singing and I'm beginning to think that the only way I will ever actually do that is to up sticks. The distance from London would force me to cut down, but I could still accept the gigs I really want to do.

Would you like to swing on a star?

First of all though, we'll have to decorate our house, which is a tip. Then we'll need to look for a job for Mark, something that he really wants to do. And when he's found a job that he really wants to do...

Carry moonbeams home in a jar?

...in an area of England in which we really want to live, we'll have to find the best schools for Michael and Abbie to grow into. And once we've achieved all that, we'll have to sell our house and find a lovely, clean, decorated house in that area. Then we will settle down to domestic bliss (fat chance)...

And be better off than you are?

...with Mark probably commuting to the nearest city, the children playing NICELY in the garden and me whiling away the hours typing psycho-science-sex-fantasies with one hand and playing Ravel on the baby grand piano with the other. What do you think?

Or would you rather have cancer?

Oh dear, I haven't mentioned the children. Well, Michael is doing very well at school and Abbie keeps announcing to anyone who will listen – such as old ladies in the street – that she and I have both got jynas but that Mummy's jyna is a big hairy one.

I do wish she wouldn't.

Write soon!!

Jx

My letters abroad stopped, abruptly, after this one. It was the last time I had so little to worry about.

What's All the Fuss?

The medical staff phoned while I was on holiday, staying with my old friend Suze in Devon. They had asked me where I could be contacted and I'd given them her number.

I'd left home the day after the mammogram, on a sunny Saturday in August. For several days I enjoyed Suze's quiet, easy life, her big house and well-behaved kids, and managed not to think about what was going on for me in Surrey.

One day Suze came out to me in the garden, worried, and said there was a message from the hospital on the answer phone. They were asking me to come in the next day to the breast clinic.

So I rang them to say I couldn't come the next day because I was on holiday. What was all the fuss about? I said I'd come the following week and put down the phone.

'Aren't you worried?' said Suze. 'I would be.'

'No. Not really,' I said. 'Nine out of ten lumps are benign. It'll be a cyst or something.'

'I'd still be worried,' she said.

I looked over at the petite harridan before me, nodding slowly with her narrowed eyes and her favourite lemon-sucking mouth, the one she always did when she was being sinister.

I wondered if maybe she was a reincarnation of the crone that accosted Julius Caesar and warned him to beware the Ides of March. Then I remembered there never was an old crone; that was Shakespeare's invention. She didn't exist. Just like this problem.

But then, Suze thought I should be worried, and Suze was usually right.

The Bell

When I got back from my short holiday on Friday 16 August, there was a message on the answer phone confirming the new appointment for the following Tuesday.

But on the Saturday a letter arrived from the hospital offering me an appointment in September.

After the weekend I rang the appointments clerk and said there must be some mistake: I had been told to come in straight away. I wasn't worried – I still wasn't worried – but neither did I want to give up my special status of being an urgent case.

'That's the earliest available appointment,' smirked the clerk. (Of course I couldn't see her, but I believe she was smirking.)

'But I've already been given an appointment for tomorrow that I think I should stick to. I think it's important that I'm seen,' I said. 'In fact the Consultant's secretary told me that my case was urgent.'

'Well, it may seem urgent to you, with respect, but she has obviously gone back to the Consultant and said that you were away and he has said that in that case it can wait for a month.'

I felt chastised. I was a silly fuss-maker. She's right, I said to myself. It's just like you to make a fuss; you're being melodramatic.

But I couldn't let it go. It wasn't quite right.

I told the girl that if she didn't mind I was going to check that out with the Consultant's secretary for myself.

'By all means,' she said. I rang the Consultant's secretary and she said, 'No. They were wrong to give away your appointment. You must come in tomorrow to the breast clinic. Mr C said that you must be seen straight away.'

I was shocked. For the first time I heard the bell toll. It was faint. But it was unmistakable.

That's what Mums are for...

The next day I turned up at the breast clinic. And waited. Of course.

Walking into hospital is like stepping back into early childhood. Once we are caught up in the vast maternal machinery of a hospital we are lost to all reason, embroiled in the myth of the welfare state. The NHS is the archetypal mother-figure. She is there just to look after us, to feed us, take away all our responsibilities and keep us safe.

The fantasy is compounded by all the little mothers: the nurses. They are ladies of indeterminate age and beauty, often curvaceous and bosomy, who scurry purposefully here and there, tending to the sick and elderly.

In the crowded, sweaty clinic, with rows of uncomfortable chairs bolted too close together and crammed with pale, frightened women and their bewildered spouses, I found myself a seat at the edge of the room so that I could rest my head against the wall and drift off to sleep. I let my mind wander back to that time when I was nurtured by another curvaceous, bosomy lady, who looked after me by right and not by rote...

1964 'Dream of Jelly Castles'

My Mum was plump – which in the 1960s was our word for horizontally-challenged – and that made me the envy of my friends with scrawnier mums.

When she cuddled me, I stayed cuddled, disappearing for a while into the big warm fat folds of her tummy. But these cuddles didn't happen often. She was always shouting at my Dad, or giving her attention to my brother and my sisters, or to the constant stream of women who came to the house looking for advice and succour, tea and sympathy. They had funny names, like Etty, Hetty and Betty; Daisy and Dora; Peggy, Polly and Dolly.

I remember her telling me not to sit on the boiler because it would give me chilblains. Of course I ignored her, and when the chilblains came and drove me crazy, she would paint them patiently every morning with red, evil-smelling liquid. Then she would bounce me up and down by the waistband of the olive-green tights that refused to climb my legs all the way to the top, so that the crotch remained stubbornly stuck just above my knees. She would bounce me right off the floor, laughing hysterically, while gravity obligingly lowered me into them, inch by inch.

If I was lucky she would walk me to school, and would sing to me: "'A' you're adorable, 'B' you're so beautiful, 'C' you're a cutiful of charms..."

I loved that, until I decided I would rather sing than be sung to, so I pulled her down to me and put my hand over her mouth, which made her laugh. Making her laugh felt good, so I did it every time she sang, until the day I accidentally hooked my little fingers onto her false teeth by mistake, pulling them out and sending them flying across the room. This was a disturbing experience that I had no wish to repeat (until I was older and began regularly begging her to dislodge them for the entertainment of my friends).

But in truth, attention from my mother was sparse, which was only to be expected with three other children and lots of needy friends to manage. So I treasured being ill. When I had a temperature or a tummy ache, my Mum would speak gently to me and stroke my forehead and sometimes even sit with me for a little while.

'Night, night,' she'd say. 'Dream of jelly castles.'

Jelly castles?

She meant well. Just as the doctors and the nurses do. And of course, I know now that she was referring to the sort of jelly castle that sits on a party table next to a chocolate cake and tastes yummy. A perfectly nice subject for a dream.

But at the time I thought she was talking about a very different kind of jelly castle. I thought she meant a fairy castle: the sort that I had seen in story books, with turrets and drawbridges, but made of jelly.

I wrestled with that misunderstanding for a long time. Whenever she said 'Night, night. Dream of jelly castles,' my heart would sink under the bedclothes. I wanted to call her back and say, 'I can't! They'll be cold and wobbly! And they won't stand up!' But I never did. Night after night I tossed and turned, struggling to create an image in my mind's eye so that I could fulfil my duty and dream about them.

After weeks of effort I finally managed to concentrate long enough to erect a feeble wreck of a castle, a bit like the ruin on the hill outside our town. As castles go, it was rubbish. Flabby and see-through, it didn't even have any light. There could never be candles in a jelly castle. Jelly melts.

But I'd done it. And there I sat in the great hall, shivering, *trapped on a small island in the dark and surrounded by choppy waters; expecting to be invaded at any moment by goodness knows what, because I knew that jelly walls would offer no protection against the wolves and giants in my fairy book, none at all...*

No, jelly castles didn't do it for me. They didn't make me feel warm or safe, and I knew deep down that neither would the NHS, being one great big jelly castle itself.

But I wanted it to, very much. And that first day in the warm, airless atmosphere of the breast clinic, the illusion of safety was strong.

I was interrupted from my reverie by a friendly Filipino nurse who sat next to me. We chatted. How strange, I remarked, that she should want to spend her day off in an outpatients' clinic. She explained that she had a cyst that needed draining.

'Why are you here?' she said.

'I have a cyst too,' I said. 'At least, I think it's a cyst.'

'There's an easy way to tell,' she said. 'Cysts are softer and move about. That's why they sometimes call them floaters.'

She probably wasn't expecting me to plunge my hand inside the neck of my top and grope about in front of all those patients but I did. I ignored them; I've always been good at ignoring things. I located the thickened area in my breast and tried to wobble it.

'Is it moving?' she asked, raising her eyebrows and nodding in that way people have of trying to get the answer they want. I couldn't give it to her. I laughed and shook my head, staring vaguely into the middle distance and still trying to wobble my

20

lump. It wouldn't move. It was thick and hard and anchored to something. My breast moved, but the lump didn't.

I gave up, removed my hand and looked around at her, my lips still stretched in a smile. But she wasn't smiling. She put her hand on my arm.

'I'm sure it will be all right.'

When did I know?

Was it then? Was it the day before, when the Consultant's secretary said, 'You must come in tomorrow'?

Was it before that, when the appointments clerk phoned me in Devon and called me in to the breast clinic?

Or before that, even? Was it the moment when the radiologists stopped their Joyce Grenfell joshing and huddled intensely over the little white stars on my mammogram?

It doesn't matter. By the time I walked into the Registrar's room for the first time, I knew in my heart that I had breast cancer.

Are You Insane?

I was momentarily distracted from my fear by the intense beauty of the Registrar. He was a relatively young man with an immoderate amount of hair. He was gorgeous. I was pleased that they had laid on a hunk for me.

Then he spoke and I went right off him.

'We've called you in here because there is something suspicious about your mammogram.'

Police jargon again, I thought.

'It may mean that we will recommend a mastectomy

and possibly some radiotherapy, and then eighteen weeks of chemotherapy. You might also need to take a hormone treatment called Tamoxifen every day for five years.'

My eyes became as big as saucers, which was good. I have always wanted eyes as big as saucers.

He explained that they needed a proper diagnosis before they could go any further and that as this was a 'one-stop' clinic, I would probably know by the end of the day whether or not I had cancer.

So there it was.

'If you have,' he said, 'we will probably offer you a mastectomy within one week.'

'A mastectomy? Why not a lumpectomy? I heard that women don't have to have mastectomies any more. They can just have the lump out.'

'That's often the case, yes; but if this is cancer it appears to be multi-focal.' I looked blank. 'I mean it's spread all over the breast,' he said. 'I mean, by the time we've...'

He was struggling. I helped him out.

'By the time you've finished excavating the site,' I said, 'there won't be anything left.'

'That's about it, yes,' he said, a little surprised at my jocularity. 'But you could have a reconstruction.'

'What's that?'

'We'll make you a new breast.'

'At the same time!?'

'We can do that, yes.'

'You mean I'll go into hospital with two dangly bits and come out with two dangly bits?'

I didn't tell him at this point about the many other dangly bits festooning my body.

'You could put it that way,' he said.

For one glorious moment it occurred to me that I might be able to 'get away with it'; that maybe I could have the operation and tell no one, since I would still have as many dangly bits as when I started. But that was madness.

I watched the Registrar reach nervously along the underside of the desk. He's looking for the panic button, I thought. He wants to set off the alarm so that the burly male nurses will come running. They'll hurl me to the ground and wrap me up in a nice comfy strait-jacket and put me in my own little magnolia-coloured room...

He remembered, at the same time as I, that this wasn't actually a psychiatric hospital. We both sighed.

'We'd like to do tests,' he said. He kept saying 'we' as if I was one of the team, but I didn't want to be. I wanted to go home and put my head under a pillow. He explained that they would reach a diagnosis in four ways: a clinical examination (hands-on); a mammogram (reshaping by steam roller); a needle aspiration (whatever that was); and maybe an ultrasound scan.

Was I going to argue?

Of course not. But my insides were arguing loudly. Inside, I didn't want to be there. I wanted to be somewhere else, in the fresh air and the sunshine. But there was no escape.

First, he felt my lumps. Then he turned me over to the student, who didn't have a clue what she was looking for and just poked at me nervously, as if she thought it might be catching.

Then he plunged a needle into my breast. He did it twice more. He called that a needle aspiration. I called it a bloody cheek. After that he said that we would have to wait for the cytology.

I waited outside; I even went to eat. When I came back the nurse with the cyst was there and remarked how strange it was that I could eat at a time like this.

'Are you insane?' I said, stuffing my face with chocolate. 'How can you not?'

Tests! We Need More Tests!

The Registrar came out, looking worried and clutching my results. He said he was just going to have a chat with the ultrasound doctor. When he came back he called me in and we all sat down again. He said that the results had come back but they were 'indeterminate' and we would have to do the needle aspiration again. He said he had asked the ultrasound doctor to do it with the needle in one hand and the ultrasound gun in the other.

Shot and stabbed at the same time, I thought.

The results, he explained, were defined on a scale of one to five; five being malignant and one being 'not enough cells to go on'. One of my lumps had come up as a 'one'. The other two had come up as 'three' and 'four'.

'What does that mean?' I said.

'Suspicious,' he said. Were we investigating a crime here?

Yes. A crime against my person, against humanity, against…

24

against… I don't know who else. There isn't anybody else is there? Only me and humanity. And maybe fairies, Father Christmas and, oh all right then, maybe God. Me, humanity, fairies, Father Christmas and God.

How did I come to believe in fairies, Father Christmas and God, when I so clearly don't believe in doctors?

There's a reason for that. And just as the hirsute young doctor was about to tell me the thing he knew about me that I fervently wished he didn't know, and wished even more fervently that he wouldn't tell, my mind flashed back to the point in my life when I 'came to believe', back to one single event in the summer of 1966, when I was nine years old.

It was the moment when Patsy Parkin and I found the gnome.

1966 The Finding of the Gnome

I had a big stick and the tree had a big hole. Patsy Parkin and I were planning something, I can't remember what, and I stuck the stick into the hole while we talked, poking down and down… and then I heard it.

'Grunt.'

'What was that?' I shrieked and pulled the stick out, examining the end for blood.

'What?' said Patsy.

'There's something in there.'

'No there isn't.'

'Yes there is, listen.' I stuck the stick in again. The thing grunted again and this time I felt a soft body give. I was scared, but not terrified: it was much too big to be a spider.

25

'I heard it,' said Patsy. We looked at each other, eyes burning bright, delighted mouths stretched wide.

'What is it,' she said.

'It must be a dwarf.'

'Why?'

'Dwarves live in trees.'

'No they don't. Dwarves live underground.'

'That is underground.'

'No it's not. It's a tree.'

'Trees go underground,' I said. Patsy tried to grab the stick but I held fast.

'Don't. You'll hurt it.'

'I won't,' she said, pulling hard. 'Let me.' So I did. She poked; it grunted and she screamed.

'What?' I said.

'It's there. It's alive!' We looked at each other for a few seconds, hardly able to believe our luck. And then I knew.

'It's a gnome,' I said. Of course! It was a gnome.

We debated telling the grown-ups, but feared that the gnome might escape while we were gone. One of us would have to stand guard until they came. And then they might do experiments on it and put it in a zoo.

Anyway it was late and getting dark. We were hungry and neither wanted to stay alone in the field with the gnome while the other fetched a grown-up.

We eventually agreed that we would come and feed it regularly, telling no one. That was best. Satisfied, we went home for our tea.

When we came the next day, dragging along a little posse of

unbelievers – not grown-ups of course – the gnome was gone. Tearfully, we thought we must have killed it with our poking the day before, until someone pointed out that it could just as easily have left home. If we could get a big stick down that hole, the gnome could get out. So we cheered up: not gnome-murderers after all.

I based my whole belief system on the finding of that gnome – believing always that there are more things in heaven and earth than are dreamt of in our philosophy – and consequently wasn't surprised one Christmas Eve when I heard, when I definitely, definitely heard the sound of hooves clattering over our roof, accompanied by the soft tinkle of jingle bells.

Because, if gnomes live in trees then witches do come out on Halloween and Father Christmas does fly through the sky every December 24 and Jesus really did once want me for a sunbeam. These things, built on the solid foundation of my gnome experience, must all be true.

And sitting there in the Registrar's office, waiting to hear the result of their horrible tests, I was hit with another kind of reality…

I realised that it must have been a squirrel.

'Ahem.' The Registrar cleared his throat and the sound brought me back into the room.

I adopted an expectant and what I believed was a hopeful face, with the somewhat desperate idea that this might influence the outcome.

'C1 means that there is no sign of cancer,' he explained again. 'C5 means that you definitely have cancer.'

'So what is mine?'

'C4.'

'So it's cancer?'

'We don't know for sure. We need to do more tests.'

'If it isn't cancer, what is it?'

'It's very unlikely not to be cancer.'

'So it *is* cancer then.'

'We don't know for sure. We need to do more tests.'

I tried another tack. I wanted to know.

'On a scale of one to ten – ten being death – where am I?' I said.

'About halfway,' he said.

Halfway towards death? I stopped thinking and feeling. We stared at each other across the desk for a while and then he picked up the phone and asked for the cancer counsellor to be paged. I could almost hear the words – unspoken – but nevertheless hanging in the air between us:

'We've got a right one 'ere.'

A Thorough Goin' Over

I was shown into a tiny room with a bed, on which I perched obediently. There was a woman with a kind face in there. She held my hand. I was annoyed and embarrassed. She was reaching inside me and trying to pull out feelings. I wasn't having any of that. I couldn't have survived my childhood if I had allowed myself to have feelings, and I was expert at denying them.

Anyway, feelings weren't appropriate in this place of dirty magnolia walls and disinfectant smells. The nurses don't care,

I thought, so why should I?

The counsellor spoke gently to me and explained that normally I would be looked after by the breast care nurse, but she was on holiday.

'Like the Consultant,' I said.

She apologized for their untimely vacations and gave me pamphlets: *Breast Cancer Care*, *Cancerbackup*, *Cancerlink*.

She asked if there was anyone I could call.

'No,' I said.

There was only Mark and he was at work. He knew I was coming to the hospital, but neither of us had allowed ourselves, even for one instant, to entertain the idea that I might actually have cancer.

Until that day at the clinic I had been pretending to myself that this was just another of my melodramas. Chronic hypochondriacs are resigned to never actually being ill.

Now it was actually happening I thought it was an outrage; a misalignment of the natural order of the Universe; a mistake of cosmic proportions.

Mark was expecting me to call, but how could I phone up and say that this time I really was ill; that I had to lose a breast; that I might die?

It would completely spoil his day.

I knew him well enough to know that he would not want to hear that I had cancer. Not over the phone. Being at work was bad enough, without that.

The counsellor mentioned family. I snorted. As if I would ever share pain with them. We had shared pain when we were little; we didn't go back there together. We never even spoke about it.

1957–1969 Feeding Time at the Zoo

My father was an alcoholic. He drank. Not all the time. He was a binge-drinker. And that made him difficult. I don't remember ever seeing him falling down drunk. But I remember stuff about my childhood that I later learned didn't happen in other people's homes.

I remember the sound of raging behind closed doors and my Mum appearing at the breakfast table with fresh bruises, which she claimed were caused by her bumping into things. She must have been very clumsy. She was always bumping into things in the night.

At the tea table, where we sat religiously every evening, my father would sometimes reach out to John and twist his ear. Red-faced and crying, John would lean towards him to minimize the pain.

Mum would yell at Dad to stop. 'You're making him lopsided! The boy's got one ear bigger than the other, because of you!' she would screech.

Of course, he didn't have one ear bigger than the other. But we believed her. We could almost see it stretching.

And sometimes plates flew through the air and hit the wall behind my mother's head.

I remember my father standing up suddenly during tea-time, calling Mum a filthy name and throwing a glass of water in her face. I vaguely remember her doing the same thing, but was that real?

When I asked my brother John about this, finally braving our familial reticence, he said that he remembers the plates flying in the other direction, towards my Dad.

John sat at my father's right hand and I sat at my mother's. My sister Jane was opposite me and my other sister Chrissie was opposite John.

So when John said he couldn't remember the plates coming down my end and I couldn't remember them flying up his end, I had a sudden vision of plates, glasses of water, items of food, salt-cellars and pepper-pots circulating elegantly in the air above our dinner table. It was all very civilized, like the laughing-gas tea-party in Mary Poppins. *Not like our family mealtimes at all.*

And did the plates of food fly both ways? Maybe in a few years, when I've plucked up the courage, I'll ask my sisters…

But not now. Not today. Today I had worse news to tell, so I certainly wasn't going to ask my eldest sister, Chrissie, about something that happened thirty years ago. She was just now dealing with the fact that her 16-year-old son had testicular cancer.

'I can't tell Chrissie,' I said aloud. 'Her son's got cancer. How can I tell her?'

At last I cried. The counsellor was satisfied. She'd done her job. And when I was mopped up she let me go for the ultrasound scan.

On the way I went straight to the nearest payphone and rang Mark after all.

'Everything's fine,' I said. 'It was nothing.'

Sounding Off

I saw someone I knew in the ultrasound waiting area, an elderly lady from my writing circle. The feelings that the counsellor had managed to prise out of me wouldn't go away. I was shocked and frightened and couldn't help vomiting the whole story over her, which seemed to make her feel shocked and frightened too. Then I felt guilty.

She told me she was a frequent visitor to the X-ray department because she had a chronic back problem. Her bad news comforted me, a bit like reading one of those shock-horror magazines, where people's brothers turn out to be half-sheep half-man and then run off to Wales with the church funds.

I commiserated with her and to her surprise said that I would rather have breast cancer. 'It's not actually hurting,' I said 'And I'll very probably recover from it completely, whereas the thought of constant back pain is… just anathema to me.'

She looked a little bemused. I babbled on. 'I mean, my illness is potentially life-threatening, but then, so is life! And I am most likely to be completely cured. And then I will be closely monitored for the rest of my life, which, if you think about it, makes me safer than the man in the street. It's also painless and not in the slightest bit debilitating. Admittedly, there's the operation, and possibly chemo, but that's only going to last, ooh, six months at the outside, and then I'll be back to normal, whereas you're in constant pain. You may never have a normal life. There's just no contest as far as I am concerned.'

She stared at me, sadly. I'm not sure my words were doing

her any good. But hey, I had cancer and I wanted revenge. That little old lady was in my path and I mowed her down with my machine gun. Rat-a-tat-tat.

'It's horses for courses,' I went on, speaking more and more quickly in a high-pitched, desperate voice. 'And if we could all choose our illnesses, then wouldn't that be a fine thing? Louise Hay says... d'you know Louise Hay?' She shook her head. 'Oh. Well, Louise Hay is a metaphysican, a celebrated metaphysician. And she says that all illnesses are due to erroneous thought patterns. Take your back, for instance.'

'My back?'

'She says that back-ache is due to lack of support. It's all very intelligently thought out. Kidney infections, for instance, are caused by being pissed off, which stands to reason when you think about it. And colds are caused by confusion. That's why they happen at Christmas, which is a very confusing time of year.

'And 'flu is caused by everyone just thinking that because it's the time of year when everyone has 'flu, they ought to have 'flu as well.

'Diarrhoea is about letting go, obviously. Pain is about guilt. And painful knees are about a fear of moving forward. Or is that toes? Anyway, diabetes is about... um... something to do with sweetness, I can't remember.'

'Having a stiff neck – or it might be shoulder – is about being a bit of a stiff; I mean, being rigid in your thinking. So think about that!'

I suddenly ran out of steam. It was a struggle, keeping that terror at bay.

'You were saying about my back?'

'I think it's financial support in the lower back and emotional support in the upper back. I'm not sure. What part of your back is in pain?'

'All of it.'

'And do you feel financially and emotionally supported?' I asked. She drew her brows together.

'Well… I'm on my own.'

'There you are then. Proof positive.'

I steamed on.

'She's written this book called *You can heal your life* and it's got all the illnesses you can possibly think of, with affirmations for how to get rid of them. She thinks that if we accept responsibility for our illnesses then we can let go of them. I mean, she thinks that we are all-powerful over our illnesses. So then, if that's true, we must be all-powerful over our "wellnesses" too.'

'Our wellnesses…' she repeated faintly.

'My word. Not hers,' I explained. She looked slightly relieved.

'There's an affirmation about cancer. And a whole chapter on it. She had it, you see.'

'Cancer? An affirmation to cure cancer? '

I faltered. It did sound a bit daft. Cancer was bigger than a cold. Quite a bit bigger. I quickly changed the subject.

'Well anyway,' I said, 'Hear this: let's say there are three different types of people in the world…'

'Only three?'

'Yeah. For my purposes, only three.' I counted them on my

fingers. 'There's type "A", the people who consider themselves to be the victim of circumstances. Yeah?'

She nodded slowly. I went on to the next finger.

'Type "B", ok? They are the people who consider themselves to be the perpetrators of their own misery and everybody else's.' She nodded again. She was getting it. Definitely getting it.

'And then there's type "C", the people who take life on the chin and just get on with it. So, roughly translated, that's:

A: "It's all your fault";

B: "It's all my fault" and

C: "What's for dinner?"'

She laughed. 'I'm the "what's-for-dinner" type,' she said.

'Are you? Hmmm,' I said, sadly. 'You probably won't get cancer then.'

I was strangely disappointed. I wanted her to be the type that says, 'It's all my fault.' The type that I was. I looked at her, devouring her ancient, lined face; staring at her wrinkles as if I had never seen such a peculiar phenomenon before. I was wondering whether I would ever get to be that wrinkly now.

After a while she spoke again.

'Well, I'm just… very, very sorry that this has happened to you,' she said.

Shocked out of my reverie by her kindness, for she really sounded as if she meant her words, I looked into her eyes and saw genuine compassion.

I had seen that look from a virtual stranger once before, when I was very young, and the force of it held me in a vice while I began to melt. To my horror the feeling that I had been trying so desperately to avoid, more painful than all my fear and anger, floated quietly to the surface.

It was shame.

1967 You're Rumbled

'You're in big trouble with Mr Dabney.'

Suze had a penny lolly, a green one, and gave it a thorough licking for dramatic emphasis. Her pink tongue stretched away from it, just as a cat's stretches away from the head of its kitten, rasping through the kitten's fur and stretching pinkly all the way back to its own mouth.

I couldn't take my eyes off it.

'Give us some,' I begged.

'No,' she said.

Why did I like Suze? She never gave me her sweets. And we were nothing alike. I was a scruff-bucket. My hair band never stayed up. I was always in trouble. And my socks fell down, all the time. Even the new ones.

Suze was the opposite. She never had a hair out of place. Her shoes were shiny, her socks didn't fall down and her jumper must have been made from a different kind of wool, since it sat in friendly folds on her little body, instead of lounging misshapen from her shoulders like mine.

In the loos that day she shook her head, enjoying my torment, and her two tight, meanly-plaited braids – straight as a die – swung out from her head like the ribbons around a maypole. Suze's Mum was a pattern-cutter. Her Dad was a draughtsman. They knew about lines. They knew about perfection. So her hair was always beautifully plaited and her skirt perfectly pleated.

She narrowed her eyes, screwed her mouth up like she was sucking a lemon, waggled the lolly at me and said:

'Aren't you worried? I would be...'

The consultation with Suze in the primary school toilets had revealed that I was in trouble for stealing a toy called a 'Slinky', egged on as usual by Patsy Parkin.

'Go on,' Patsy had said, nudging me painfully with her elbow. 'I dare you.' I had hesitated, appalled at the enormity of the crime.

'You haven't got the guts,' she said, and turned away.

That stung me. I did have guts; that was the one thing I did have. You had to develop guts to survive in our house. So I picked it up and marched out of the shop without looking back, not once. And Patsy, even wicked Patsy Parkin, was impressed.

I wanted everyone to be impressed. I liked admiration, the admiration I got from my peers when I ran the fastest, danced the best or fought with the boys; admiration that I never received at home or from the teachers. That's why I boasted about it, boasted that this time I had not stolen a penny sweet, which was a commonplace crime amongst the naughty children, but a whole toy, a toy in its own box, which was worth as much as half-a-crown.

Oh yes, I had entered the big league.

It was a wondrous creation, made of shiny metal bangles that joined up magically so it jangled like a gypsy's wrist as it marched under its own power down the stairs. The loud jingling chatter of the coils brought everyone from all over the house to admire the toy. And I basked in their approval – my brother, my sisters and my parents – approving of me, for once the bringer of beauty. It was a thing so shining, so noisy and clever; an intelligent stack of metal coils that could walk downstairs on its own.

'Where did you get that?' laughed my Mum.

'Lavinia Davenport lent it to me.' I delivered the fateful line that I had rehearsed carefully all the way home.

'Who's Lavinia Davenport?'

'Nobody. Just a girl.'

But she wasn't just a girl. She was trouble. She had friends.

'Mary Wickman and Jill Smith are going to Mr Dabney and gonna tell him what you did to Lavinia Davenport.'

'I only said I borrowed the Slinky from her.'

'She thinks you're saying she stole it.'

'I never said that. I only said I borrowed it.'

'Well, stupid,' said Suze, not a sympathetic child at the best of times, 'how would she be able to lend it to you if she hadn't stolen it from The Toy Box herself?'

She put the lolly back in her mouth while I chewed over her words. I had nothing else to chew on. If I had some boiled sweet taste in my mouth, I thought, I would have felt stronger.

But there was no lolly and no escaping my fate. When I left the school at the end of the day a small committee of 'good girls' blocked my way. They announced that if I didn't tell my parents that evening that it was I who had stolen the Slinky toy and not poor, innocent Lavinia, they would be telling on me tomorrow. There was no room for negotiation. The game was up.

I staggered home, burdened with fear and shame; turning from white to scarlet and then back again as my painful feelings assailed me.

When I was very quiet and wouldn't eat my tea, even my mother noticed and asked me what was wrong. Sobbingly I told her.

'We must tell the Old Man,' she said, 'and we'll do nothing until he gets home.' She went to the telephone and summoned my father early from work, which was a rare enough occurrence to ensure his swift arrival.

I heard them mumbling outside the bedroom door and, despite my tears, rejoiced at the sound of level-toned discourse between my parents, which was not a sound I was accustomed to hearing.

Dad came into the room, holding the Slinky in its box. I had owned it for two weeks by now and no longer thought it so fine. In fact, after the first few times it seemed like a silly game to play. So I wasn't fretting at the idea that it would be taken away from me. In fact I wanted it to be, along with the lies and the guilt and my criminal record.

'Come on,' he said and off we went. I walked quickly by his side, hopping and skipping to keep up with him as usual. I was astonished that we were out on a jolly on such a terrible day and asked him where we were going.

'Just for a walk,' he said. I cheered up and chattered happily at him, having no idea where we were going until we stopped suddenly outside the Toy Box.

'Come on,' he said, again, and before my body could register resistance and begin to work in the opposite direction, he pushed into the shop and dragged me firmly behind him.

It was a large shop, cool and dark with wooden shelves, but brightened by rows and rows of gleaming toys.

There were a few customers, but it must have been near closing time as there were no children. All the good little children were far away, playing outside their happy homes in the late afternoon sunshine.

My Dad marched up to the counter and put the Slinky down.

'I'm sorry to have to tell you that my daughter is a thief.' He spoke loudly. Heads snapped in our direction. 'She stole this ridiculous toy from you a couple of weeks ago and I would like to pay for it.'

Every customer in the shop stopped talking and looked at me. Some appeared around the ends of the shelving units to get a better view.

I drowned in shame. I hung my head, clinging to the skirt of my school pinny with both hands and staring at the floor, wishing so hard that I could melt into a puddle and slip away over the lino – not jangling proudly like the silver bangles of the Slinky – but sliding noiselessly across the grubby surface and under the nearest shelf, out of sight and out of the astonished gaze of that shopkeeper.

'Of course I'll pay you for it, but we need to know whether or not you are going to call the police to come for her.'

I looked up at my Dad. Was he serious? Was he really going to let me go to prison? My heart stopped.

The shopkeeper leaned heavily on the counter for support and looked down. He smiled a little smile and winked at me.

I saw kindness, forgiveness, compassion and a deep love for children in that man's eyes. I saw a different world, where children lived without the companionship of fear and shame.

*I decided that I liked the shopkeeper and felt shabby that I
had stolen from him. And then he spoke.*

*'Oh, well,' he said, 'I don't think so. If she's sorry.' I couldn't
believe my ears. He was prepared to save me from the hangman's
rope, though my own father would not.*

My Dad looked down at me. 'Are you sorry?' he asked.

'Yes,' I whispered, and nodded my head.

*'Then we'll say no more about it,' said the shopkeeper. And
that was that.*

Back in the ultrasound waiting room, when the old lady looked
at me with that same abundance of compassion in her eyes, I
had the same terror that I was going to melt, to dissolve into
a puddle of hot shameful tears on the floor of the crowded
waiting room and slide out of the door. But this time I wasn't
going to be let off the hook so easily. I had cancer. Exactly
why I felt so ashamed of that, I didn't yet know, but I was sure,
somehow, that it was all my fault.

I appealed silently to the God of my childhood to forgive me
for whatever it was I'd done to deserve this blight and to take
it away; to let me slip through the net just one more time. But
answer came there none and before I could start crying again,
the ultrasound nurse appeared and dragged me to her lair.

Inside the little room I was asked to strip off my upper
half. Then I was smeared with jelly and examined by the
equipment.

The hand that held the equipment was attached to the arm
of the female ultrasound doctor, who was too thin and also, I
decided, emotionally dysfunctional.

She had the ultrasound gun in one hand and a large needle in the other, which she jabbed once into my breast and said, 'It's a wrap,' or something like that.

I grabbed her arm, to which she took great exception.

'What about the other lumps?' I said. 'There are three.'

'Well… we have a good biopsy there, and we will have enough material from that lump to get a diagnosis. The others are too small.' She tried to pull away but I held fast.

'But I'm sure the Registrar said it would make the difference between whether or not I lose my whole breast,' I said, unruly tears escaping down my cheeks. 'If the other lumps are just cysts, maybe,' I said, 'then I might only have to have the big lump out.'

I wanted to save my breast. I was only 39, too young for this to be happening. And even if they were moving gradually towards Australia, I was proud of my breasts; they were beautiful. I didn't want a mastectomy. I didn't want any of this to be happening to me.

But I was clutching at straws and also at her arm, which she wanted back. She looked down at my hand and back up at my wet face.

'I don't think that will be the case,' she said, casually squeezing my heart with her words. 'Whatever those lumps are, they are all the same.'

20 August 1996

Dear Dr A,

Thank you for referring this 39-year-old lady to the breast clinic, where I saw her on Mr C's behalf today.

She presented to you, I understand, about two weeks ago with a two-week history of a tender left breast lump and a subsequent mammogram three days later was reported as showing three suspicious lesions. She tells me now the lump has become more tender. She has no particular risk factors for breast disease.

On examination today there was a lumpy area with two discreet lumps, lateral to the left nipple. The more medial one was a bit harder and pea-shaped and the lateral one was slightly less well defined. I attempted a fine needle aspiration today but unfortunately had an inadequate sample on the medial one and a suspicious sample on the second.

Unfortunately this has not given us a firm diagnosis. I discussed the situation with Dr G and she is going to attempt to do an ultrasound guided fine needle aspiration this afternoon.

I will see Janice next week and I have obviously had a long chat with her. She has also spoken to our palliative care nurse, who is standing in for our breast care nurse. It may be that we might need to do some wire localisation in this lady. I will discuss the situation with her next week.

Yours sincerely
Dr F,
Registrar to Mr C, Consultant Surgeon

'Whatever Those Lumps Are, They Are All the Same'

I picked the children up from my friend Julie's house – saying nothing to her about what was happening – and took them home. They ran upstairs and I sat down on the sofa. After ten minutes of staring into space I was interrupted by Michael, bursting into the room with Abbie in tow.

Michael was crazy about Captain Scarlett – whom he called 'Sackitt Cap' – and had invented his own superhero, 'Knicker Man', which involved him wearing his underpants on his head so that the leg-holes became eye-holes. It was a strange kind of balaclava. I cheered and correctly identified Abbie as Knicker Man's sidekick, 'Sock Girl', as she was wearing socks on her hands and feet.

I watched them parade about, whilst I sat surreptitiously poking and prodding the offending breast, trying not to feel the lumps that were so obviously there.

And while I smiled and clapped the children's antics, inside I cried.

The Cat Comes out of the Bag

The next hurdle was telling Mark.

When I met Mark he was a resting actor and spent his days piddling about on the Amstrad, making up computer programmes that created white trees on a black screen or black trees on a white one. I confronted him with this latent geekiness and forced him to find a support group, which he called a degree in Computing and Information Technology.

He had only recently graduated, which meant that things were going to get easier for us financially at last, and now, at

44

the end of the very first day in his shiny new well-paid job as an IT Consultant, I had to tell him I had breast cancer.

I loved Mark. He was my husband and the father of my children, but he wasn't great in a crisis. When the going got tough, he got going, for sure. But it was usually in the opposite direction. Years before, I'd returned after a car crash and he'd made it all about him, leaving me bruised and shaken while he went upstairs to deal with his painful feelings.

So I wasn't looking forward to telling him about this biggest crisis in our marriage to date. And as I had suspected, he did not take it well.

He was shocked. He was angry. He pointed out that he'd just started a new job.

So on the day when we should have been sharing the burden of this terrible news together, I withdrew, going upstairs to be alone. I couldn't deal with Mark's upset feelings just then.

I needed to be selfish.

Blaming God

The next day, Wednesday, was horrible. I went to fetch Michael from school and was exhausted by the time I got home. The stress of not telling other people until I knew for sure was overwhelming.

I let myself in and did my chores. As soon as Mark came home and could take over with the children, I escaped to the bathroom, where I stood and looked at my naked breasts in the mirror for a long while. Then I ran myself a bath and locked the door. We didn't usually lock the door.

Lying in the warm water I cried; really cried, at last. I

wept for fear of the future and for the breast that they were going to take away. I loved my breasts. I was hurt that God was going to do this thing to me. What did I do to deserve this, I asked, when I had cried myself out and was casting around for someone to blame. My inner voice answered.

'You did it to yourself. You ate too much, drank too much, smoked and stressed and fussed and fretted your whole life through. And now look. You only have yourself to blame.'

My thoughts turned again to God, that long-neglected friend. Could the voice have come from Him? No, that vicious self-critic cannot be God, I thought, any more than He can be the witty voice that sometimes speaks to me.

On the other hand… if there is no God at all, I thought, then we are all just mice in frock-coats, scurrying frantically about; pointlessly trying to control a hostile and uncontrollable universe.

The voice spoke up again. 'Do you remember the story of the Fisherman's Wife by the Brothers Grimm?'

Not waiting for an answer, He steamed ahead.

'She and her husband lived in a miserable hovel by the sea. Then one day her husband caught a magic fish and let it go and it promised him wishes. But his wife was never satisfied. First she wanted a pretty cottage, then a castle. Then she wanted to be King, then Emperor, then Pope; and finally she wanted to be God. And the magic fish got pissed off, at last, and sent them back to their hovel.'

I was not in the mood for parables. 'There was no fish,' I said. 'You were the fish.'

God didn't reply. I relented. 'Ok. What are you trying to say? Do I have a castle? No. I do not.'

'I'm trying to say,' God said quietly, and gently, as God is wont to do, 'that maybe it's important that you keep losing what you already have until you begin to be grateful for it.'

I understood at last. He wanted me to count my blessings, because He knew that I could.

I got out of the bath and went through my papers until I found it: something I'd written the year before for a competition. I slid back into the warm water and read it again, knowing that the message it bore had turned out to be chillingly prophetic.

The Incident of the Three-Legged Pram

I was puffing and panting down Hook Road in Epsom, bemoaning my fate as usual. Abbie, very small at the time, was lying flat inside the old pram and it was cold, so the blue gabardine flap was raised and stretched a little way up the hood to shield her from the wind. At least she is comfy-cosy, I thought, as I battled to push the pram against the wind, pulling toddler Michael along behind me.

He began to shriek and wouldn't walk, but I was more determined. The traffic was heavy and I couldn't let him go. He must walk or die. I was dragging Michael with one hand and pushing the pram with the other. So I was already feeling very sorry for myself when one of the wheels fell off.

I didn't move for a minute as I assessed the situation: a heavy lopsided pram in one hand and a suicidal toddler in the other, and that minute was just long enough for someone, somewhere, to decide that it really ought to be hailing, even though it was May.

We'd had five years of rotten luck: redundancy followed by unplanned, mistimed children, unplanned and mistimed exotic illnesses, broken limbs, burglaries and vicious cars, amongst other misfortunes. And now this insult: a three-legged pram in the hail.

'Excuse me; do you have a spanner by any chance?' I asked a passer-by, politely.

'Why?' she said, so I showed her the pram and explained my plan for mending it. 'No. Sorry,' she said, and went on her way.

'You could still push it, you know,' said another passer-by. 'Just lean on it.' And she was right. I picked Michael up and sat him on the outside cover, using his weight to balance the pram so that it would move without toppling over. It worked. Great joy suddenly overwhelmed me. It's hailing and my pram has only got three wheels, I thought, but I can still walk.

Laughing, I shook my fist at the grey sky and shouted, 'At least I can still walk! You can't take that away from me!' I marched off down the road and into a new life, because I knew I had discovered something really important.

That night, I tried to explain it to my husband.

'The Kingdom of Heaven is at hand,' I said.

'Oh dear,' he said, because he knew me well.

'I mean, what if an Angel knocks at the door tonight and tells you that he has come for your legs…'

'Come for my legs!'

'Yes, what if he has come for your legs and you are not going to have any legs after that moment?'

'And that's the Kingdom of Heaven, is it?'

'No. It's this. The point of that line from the Bible is that true happiness is at our fingertips.'

'I see. No legs?'

'Or arms, or eyes, or prams.'

'Prams!'

'Yes, supposing he said that you weren't going to have these things any more, how would you feel about the way you have spent today? Would you be happy with the things that you have said and done?'

He didn't answer, but I could see that he was impressed.

'And supposing this Angel comes and says this was your last day on earth? Would you be happy with the way you've spent it?'

I told him then about the three-legged pram and the hail, and how I had triumphed over adversity completely and forever from that instant, because I had realised that it is only here and now and this moment that matters, and counting your blessings, your real blessings, like your health and your children: not money and cars but realising what you've got and loving every minute of it, and knowing that if they take one, or two, or all the wheels from your pram, or legs from your body, then at least you can still see, or hear, or talk, or write, or whatever you've got left, and that's the great glory and joy of being alive!

I told him all of this and he said, 'That's very good. It's even true. But can you keep it up?'

'Of course I can.'

And so I did. For a whole week, I didn't moan once. That's not bad is it? And even if I do moan occasionally, I know I will never be the same again, after that moment when I got my three-legged pram to walk.

I put the pages down and stared into the gloom. The water was cooling off and it was getting late. Mark knocked on the door.

'Are you all right?'

Mark didn't believe in any of this 'crazy stuff'. I knew I couldn't share my thoughts with him.

'I want to be alone,' I said.

Lying in the tepid water, I wondered if the experience with the pram was some kind of premonition. Or was it a gift, like the phial of magic light the good fairy gives to the princess to guide her through the dark times ahead?

Or was it just a complete coincidence?

Either way, the Angel hadn't come for me that night, or that week, or for a whole year. And when it did come, it didn't take the wheels from my pram or the legs from my body.

It took my breast.

Cancer? Oh No! What will the Neighbours Think?

The next day, Michael's fifth birthday, was the day of the party.

Mr Sausages was making the children laugh with the 'knickers' word, while I poured blackcurrant and orange juice into plastic cups and my friend Penny the nurse asked me if I'd had a nice summer.

I told her I had breast cancer. She put her hand on my arm and said, 'You must let me help you.'

And so it began.

In the first few days, it seemed to me that telling people about my cancer was giving them too much information. It was like suddenly appearing in public with my knickers on the outside of my trousers. I had told Penny and the lady from my writing circle, the one I bumped into at the hospital, but I hadn't told anyone else. I knew I would have to now. Friends. Relatives. Strangers. It worried me. I thought it would upset them and that it would be my fault. Ludicrous as it might sound, I was even worrying by this time what the neighbours would think.

I come from a generation who were taught never even to mention cancer. If we spoke of it at all, we would call it 'The Big C', whispering its name in furtive huddles, knowing that anyone unlucky enough to have it would probably soon be dead.

These attitudes start young and stay deep. I was ashamed of having cancer. I felt… wrong. I felt like John Hurt's character in *Alien* must have felt when the monster bursting from his stomach broke up the lunch party. Well ok, maybe not quite that bad. But it was embarrassing, like admitting to having nits.

I was in shock. And as a defence, part of me struggled to stay flippant.

There is an emotional process, defined by a Swiss doctor called Elisabeth Kubler-Ross, called the Grief Cycle. It goes like this: shock, denial, anger, bargaining, depression, testing and acceptance. People can get stuck in one phase. I'm not sure I ever got all the way through it, but I certainly sat for a long time in denial, which manifested itself in crazy, disassociated imaginings and looked an awful lot like bravery. It wasn't.

I couldn't have cancer, I thought. Where I come from,

it is one of those things that we must avoid at all costs. We mustn't be successful, we mustn't be a political campaigner and we mustn't be ill. And we definitely must not walk around wearing brightly coloured scarves that sit far too snugly on our bald heads above our ghostly-white faces, demanding sympathy and attention.

The very idea!

I was terrified of this inappropriateness. Being the centre of attention was wonderful when it was a celebration of my usefulness or talent or beauty, but being the centre of attention because I was ill was quite a different kettle of fish.

I tried to be rational. Cancer, I thought, is just a simple matter of cell reproduction gone wild. Just like warts. But warts are not pleasant whichever way you look at them. And if cancerous tumours are warts, they're bloody big ones.

I tried it out in my head.

'Yes,' I would say to the Mums in the playground, 'what you've heard on the school grapevine is true. I do have cancer. But don't worry, it's just like having warts. Large, internal ones.'

I realised that wasn't going to work, not to mention the fact that I would scare to death any actual wart-sufferers who were unlucky enough to ask after my health.

What was happening to me wasn't pretty. It wasn't nice. In fact, it just wasn't on.

I was only 39.

I'm too young for this, I said. But no one was listening.

I remembered being in this place before...

There was another time in my life when I was too young

to deal with bad behaviour from my body, another time when I was the first amongst my peers to have something nasty growing in my pantry.

1968 The Curse of Womankind

'Women who began having periods early (before age 12) ...
have a slightly increased risk of getting breast cancer.'
The American Cancer Society

One day I was a child – a strong child, throwing boys around like confetti – and the next I was a weak, mewling creature with a shirt that wouldn't lie straight on my chest. Two nasty bumps had appeared. When I complained about the little mounds to some older children on the estate, they taunted me, pointing at my chest and calling, 'Fried eggs!'

I laughed along with them but hated the idea that my breasts were not up to scratch. Patsy Parkin and I consoled ourselves with the idea that those 'mature' girls – the ones with the large breasts – were over-ripe.

'They're peaking early,' we used to say. 'Soon they will look like old ladies with their huge breasts dangling down to their waists and the boys won't want them.'

We were convinced that breasts went on growing at the same rate as they appeared, which in most cases was violently sudden.

I hated puberty altogether. I lost control of my body. From being a skinny ten-year-old, I grew enormous hips and little bumps on my chest. Then my legs suddenly shot up, so that the torso seemed to be even more squashed together. My socks and skirt were suddenly too short; there was a great white expanse of leg between them. I felt awkward and clumsy and suffered horribly from cheeks that blushed at the slightest attention and were a different colour red from my hair.

Me, 2nd from right, hating puberty

And I missed out on sex education. It happened one day when I was off school with a cold. My school friends didn't tell me anything. Neither did my sisters. My Mum never got around to the kindly chat I'm sure she was planning. So that was that.

One day, the year before, she had marched into the house with the cartoonishly grim mouth that she favoured on serious occasions, and tossed a couple of booklets at my brother and me as we sat at the kitchen table.

'You'd better read those,' she said and left the room in a hurry, perhaps fearing awkward questions.

If either of us had been alone we might have been tempted to pick up those booklets, and who knows what difference that would have made; but as it was, we looked at each other, brother and sister, thirteen and ten; we looked at the booklets, which were obviously about something bad that the grown-ups knew, and without a word we tossed them into the bin. Tacitly we agreed to hold on to our innocence a little while longer.

That was a mistake.

My mother, believing that the nasty issue of sex education was now dealt with, never raised the subject again. So when I started to notice brown stains in the front of my knickers a year later, I was puzzled. Day by day, they became redder and redder, and I saw what could only be described as blood on the loo paper. I was terrified. I was bleeding inside. Somewhere inside, I thought, I must have been cut.

I went down to my Mum in the kitchen straight away. There would have to be an ambulance, I thought, like the one that took away Mr Smith from next door when he had a heart attack. They took him out on a stretcher, the sheet pulled up over his head, and he never came back.

I tugged at my Mum's sleeve. She was washing up but looking over her shoulder and talking to someone else, I don't remember who. It could have been the Queen for all I cared. I needed to interrupt. 'Mum,' I whispered, pulling her ear down to my mouth. 'I'm bleeding inside. I'm bleeding to death.'

She looked shocked for a few seconds and then the penny dropped.

'Oh,' she said, a brief look of relief flitting over her face. Then, grim again, she wiped her hands on a tea-towel and said, 'You'd better come with me.' I followed her out of the room and up the stairs. I was relieved but also felt that I must have done something wrong. She was so stern, so cross.

She locked us in the bathroom and took something out of the

cabinet that looked like a bandage but not quite. It was a ball of something that unrolled into a long flat thing, about six inches in length, with two loops at the end. My Mum handed it to me and let me feel the pad of compressed cotton wool, tightly held in shape by cotton net. 'You'll be needing this,' she said. 'This is a sanitary towel. And this is what you do.'

She still looked severe. I felt that I had let the family down somehow, but was glad that I wasn't being asked to pack my bags, although from the look on her face it was touch-and-go. She handed me a pink elastic belt which, I think, also had loops; it was so long ago, it's hard to remember now. You don't see any 1960s sanitary belts in the glass cases of the British Museum. She put it around my waist and it was so big it slipped down to my hips. She had to put it on the smallest setting. Then she showed me how to dangle the pad between my legs and fix it to the belt with safety pins: one at the front and one at the back.

'What's it for?' I said.

'To catch the blood.'

'What's wrong with me?' I whispered. I didn't want to wear the thing. It was huge and ugly. It felt like a horse's bridle on me. I had been caught and tamed and nothing would ever be the same again. I was right.

'It's your period,' she said. 'Didn't you read that booklet I gave you?' I remembered how John and I had looked at each other and laughed as we tossed the two little books in the bin.

'No.' I shook my head, ashamed at my foolishness. Mum tutted. 'You'll have to tell the teacher,' she said. 'You mustn't shower when you've got your period. And you mustn't walk *about with nothing on your feet. Your passageways will all be open and you'll get a cold in your kidneys.'*

'I don't want to wear this,' I said. My Mum snorted.

'You're lucky,' she said, handing me some clean knickers. 'We used to have to sew them with cotton and lint.'

The next day I told the games mistress, carefully following my Mum's instructions, though the shame was excruciating.

'Please can I be excused, Miss, because I've got my period.'

She nearly passed out with horror. She looked furtively over her shoulder. 'You don't have to say that,' she hissed. 'Just say that you want to be excused.'

Unlike the games mistress, the head teacher at the big, old-fashioned girls' grammar school was new and progressive. On her first day she told us that we must stop kneeling to say our prayers. This was helpful, because it was quite common for at least one girl to faint upon standing up, and the hall was so crowded that whoever fainted usually took a few other girls down with her.

She also abolished the posture lessons and the detentions handed out for being seen in the town with our scarves over the wrong shoulder or our berets at the wrong angle.

And not long after my periods started, she shocked the whole school by revealing that some girls were stuffing their sanitary towels behind the toilet, rather than face the embarrassment of coming out of the cubicle with them and walking across to the bin, which she didn't seem to think was a good idea. If only she had made that announcement a few weeks earlier, I would have asked someone what the hell she was talking about.

'What is a sanitary towel?' I might have said. And maybe someone would have told me.

They were different times. I'm sure my Mum wasn't really cross; she was probably sad for me and doing the best she could. Anyway, it's not surprising that her ways were a little eccentric.

After all, she was brought up by my Nan.

1957-1968 The Wisdom of the Elders

Nan was old and had three teeth and a few wisps of hair that she coiled into a bun at the top of her head with a Kirby grip. She was built like a cottage loaf and in fact lived in a real country  *cottage with a thatched roof and roses around the door. She seemed very old and scary to me, but she was definitely nicer than her friend Maud, who smelled strongly of disinfectant.*

When Maud came to the cottage I would hide under the table and couldn't be persuaded to come out.

Nan was looked after by an Irishman called Paddy who spoke with an incomprehensible accent and kept a wonderful vegetable garden out the back.

We visited Nan once a month without fail. It was a two-hour bus ride. We'd get off at the war monument in the village and walk up the lane past the graveyard with the pretty latch gate where Granddad was buried. From there we could see the cottage at the top.

It was a tedious journey. I was invariably sick on the bus and then sometimes when we got there Nan would try to stop us coming in. She was easily confused and thought Mum was 'from the welfare'.

Inside, I would run straight through to the kitchen and swing on the back door. It had a latch and a shelf at the bottom that you could stand on if you were very small. If you pushed off with your foot it would swing you out into the garden. I would do it for as long as I could until Paddy spotted me and chased me away. The cottage was a happy place. There was always noise and clutter, and I would creep back and swing on the door and marvel at Paddy's Irish lilt, which I thought was more like singing than talking.

Sometimes Nan would sing too. She claimed to have been an opera singer, though Mum said that wasn't true. But she sounded like one to me, sitting me on her knee and singing about my tiny hand being frozen, though I assured her repeatedly that it wasn't, which made her laugh.

Other times, she would tell me stories.

She told me that she had been a waitress, and about the man who came in just before closing time and asked for eight glasses of water, one after the other, which she had delivered with a cheery smile every time. 'Do you know what he left me for a tip?' she would say, and I would shake my head, though of course I did know, having heard the story a dozen times: 'He left me a gold sovereign. A whole gold sovereign.'

I understood that this was the right way to behave: that I should keep serving up the glasses of water without complaint; and that if I was lucky I might get a whole gold sovereign to keep for myself. I saw it as a metaphor for life, young as I was.

She told me how her Great Uncle Dick had owned a boot shop and one day a horse and cart had driven into it, right through the window.

And how my Granddad, who died before I was born, had been a tram-driver.

And how Uncle Dick sometimes took out his glass eye and dropped it into men's beers in bars when he wanted to start a fight.

And how my Mum's sister Elsie had died in a motorcycle accident in 1928, having first given birth to twins that were so small they'd been put into a shoebox until the undertaker came to take them away.

And how Uncle Dick had eventually hanged himself with the lavatory chain, as if it were quite understandable that he should do so.

She told me wonderful stories like that.

So it is not surprising that I believed Nan completely when she explained to me one day the mystery of menstruation.

My Mum must have told her my news, for the very next time we visited she took me aside and whispered, 'It is the curse, dear, that's all.'

'What curse?' I asked.

'God punished Eve for persuading Adam to eat the apple,' she said. 'You know your Bible stories?'

I nodded.

'Well, women have been paying for Eve's sin ever since,' she said. 'God threw them out of the Garden of Eden and said that women would be cursed forever after with labour, with giving birth in terrible pain, and with bleeding every month. It's God's curse on womankind and quite right too.'

Oh well, I said to myself, there you are then. It is the curse of womankind. Fair enough.

27 August 1996

Dear Dr A

Further to my previous letter in this complicated situation I reviewed Janice again today. We have not got a full diagnosis with the fine needle aspiration of what appeared to be multifocal carcinomas in her left breast on mammogram. The ultrasound guided FNA last week was C4 which is a highly suspicious carcinoma. However, as I say these do look particularly suspicious on mammogram.

We have had a long chat with Janice, who wants to get as much information as possible before deciding what needs doing, and we have explained to her that it is very likely she may well need a mastectomy. She tells me she is extremely keen on immediate reconstruction.

I still feel that we need to get a tissue diagnosis and therefore I did a true cut biopsy of the main palpable lump left of her left nipple. We also repeated some mammograms with lateral and paddle views.

Our plan is that she will go to the combined clinic when our colleagues are here this coming Thursday so that she can get as much information about the medical treatment of breast cancer as possible and then she is going to see Mr C in a week's time in his clinic on Thursday to decide treatment.

Yours sincerely

Dr F

Registrar to Mr C

'Doctor, Doctor, it hurts when I do this.' 'Don't do it then.'

Despite my protestations that I would have no more mammograms ever, I now meekly submitted to two. The time for jokes was past and I had more than a mammogram to worry about. I also had a big fat needle biopsy under local anaesthetic, which is to say that the doctor harpooned me and tore out a little strip of tissue to analyse.

And an official diagnosis? Oh come on, that would have been too easy. They said that until the Consultant returned from holiday, they wouldn't give me the final picture and what was to be done about it, though I knew it, even if they didn't. As it turned out, they were by this time talking about it quite happily amongst themselves.

29 August 1996

Dear Dr A

I reviewed this lady in the joint breast clinic today. You will recall that she presented with a left breast nodule and was found to have multi-focal disease on mammography. True cut biopsy showed grade 2 invasive ductal carcinoma and I have told her the biopsy result today.

The standard treatment in this situation is a mastectomy and she will be seeing Mr C himself in the next week or so to plan surgery. Because the tumour is grade 2, irrespective of nodal status we would advise adjuvant chemotherapy and no doubt we will see her here in due course to consider this.

It is most likely we will offer participation in the TRAFIC trial which compares bolus with protracted venous infusion treatment. She will also require Tamoxifen. Radiotherapy will be decided on the basis of surgical findings.

We discussed all of the treatment that she will receive in some detail today and no doubt Mr C will keep you informed of her progress in the next few weeks.

Yours sincerely

Mr H, SR to Dr I

The Sprit of No!

Before Mr C returned, I took control of my destiny and asked them if they could make a new breast out of my fat belly, killing two birds with one stone.

'No,' said the chemo Registrar.

'No,' said the cancer Registrar.

'No,' said the breast nurse.

63

That would be a 'No' then, I thought.

They said it had to be reconstructed from the Latisimuss Dorsi muscle from the back, just behind the breast. They would bring it round, still attached, so that it had its own blood supply. When it had healed up, I would have two breasts.

At this point, imbued with the spirit of 'No,' I considered saying 'No' to the reconstruction. Refusing the mastectomy never actually occurred to me. The cancer was there and it needed to be cut out. That much was obvious. But what about the reconstruction? What if I didn't have that?

A friend told me that his aunt had survived breast cancer with a mastectomy and no reconstruction. She wore a prosthesis – a falsie – stuffed inside her bra.

She agreed to speak to me and when I rang she told me a funny story.

She said she had danced once with a man who made it clear that he admired her womanly shape. He went so far as to whisper in her ear that she had beautiful breasts. So she fished out her prosthesis and handed it to him, saying that if he was that fond of it, perhaps he'd like to take it home. I laughed, but not that much. Though I admired that lady for her ability to laugh about her lost breast, I didn't think I could handle that; and I knew Mark wouldn't be able to handle it either. He wouldn't be able to handle it because it wouldn't be there. B'boom.

I could make jokes too.

Flippancy had rescued me from many a painful experience in my life and I turned to it again, digging out a notebook and writing on the cover: 'Getting Abreast of Things.' Then I wrote in it: '*So now it is officially declared that I have breast cancer and that the breast will have to come off, as the actress said to the bishop.*'

Of course the actress never said any such thing. But it amused me, and I needed to be amused.

The next day I was on the phone all morning, ringing the numbers from the pamphlets that the counsellor had given me.

'I'm concerned about how to tell the children,' I said, to the adviser at Cancerbackup, whilst Abbie played at my feet. 'I mean, I might die, mightn't I? And I need to break it to them gently.' Abbie was three and a half and could probably understand me perfectly well. I think, perhaps, I wasn't firing on all four cylinders.

The phone operatives from the organizations were warm and caring and said that they would send me information. One volunteer from Cancerlink gave me the telephone number of a contact for my nearest support group. I rang that lady and had a long chat. She said there was a self-help group not too far away that met every Tuesday, and she shared some of her own experiences as a cancer survivor

Her husband had died from cancer and she had nursed him. Then she got cancer herself. Then someone's leg fell off. Then her grown-up son was badly injured, narrowly escaping death.

It was a long and shocking history of one misfortune after another and cheered me up no end.

The Ladies with the Scarves

'Hope is the thing with feathers
that perches in the soul
that sings the tune without the words
and never stops at all'
Emily Dickinson

I took the breast care nurse's advice and went to visit her Cancer Support Group at the hospital. They were brave ladies with scarves on their heads and symptoms caused by chemotherapy, such as mouth ulcers, hair loss, nausea and hand-sores.

But the ladies were fear-filled and allowing that fear to feed on itself, to multiply and hover in the room like a thick black cloud, while they discussed the merit of different wigs and how few mouth ulcers they had in comparison to their neighbours.

And not an ounce of hope between them. Only sad, brave smiles.

I'm not saying all the NHS support groups are like that. Just that one, on that particular morning.

I didn't go again.

The Mavericks

The NHS group hadn't worked for me but I knew I needed a support group of some sort. I thought of the lady whose relatives had all been assailed by misfortune. Despite her troubles she had still managed to sound genuinely jolly. I dug out her directions and drove deep into the country to find the support group she had recommended.

The group was like the Mad Hatter's tea party in *Alice in Wonderland*. They didn't make light of the disease; they just made light of life. And that's what I needed. After all, don't angels fly because they take themselves lightly? I ate cake, drank tea and one by one I heard the members' stories.

One middle-aged lady had been diagnosed with cancer seventeen years before. She had walked out of the hospital after the first appointment and never gone back, having been given only a few months to live. 'I'm still here,' she said proudly. I asked her why she kept coming to the group, why she didn't want to put it all behind her. 'It's mine, that's why,' she said. 'It's my cancer. No one is going to take it away from me.'

Another was a hypnotherapist whose daughter had been wrongly diagnosed with cancer and unnecessarily operated upon. He was full of rage against drug- and surgery-based treatment, and sat harrumphing and spitting out alternative remedies like some deranged one-armed bandit that has decided to make everyone a winner.

Several of them didn't think much of orthodox treatment. Some had even refused it and had lived to tell the tale. I was astounded. Refused the treatment?! Was that even allowed?

One little old lady who had survived bowel cancer for many years sported an eye-patch that reminded me of swashbucklers and pirates.

I was thrilled! Hadn't I swashbuckled my way through school? I missed the excitement of my pirating days. My situation suddenly took on the appearance of an adventure. I was still in deadly danger but it was in the realm of chaos and drama that I knew well, that I had grown up in; a million miles away from the quiet, sensible desperation of the ladies with the scarves.

There are different strokes for different folks, but that strange little bunch of mavericks at the cancer support group stroked me back to life. They were a merry band of pirates, some of them outlawing themselves from conventional treatment and all of them sailing the high seas with a 'yo-ho-ho and a bottle of rum!'.

My favourite was an American lady called Val, a real rebel, who wheezed with emphysema and claimed to be having a double mastectomy – a bilateral, it was called – 'for the sake of symmetry'.

She also said she was having a reconstruction made from her abdominal flesh and muscles. What was that, I thought. Did I hear her right? A breast made from her fat tummy? I was excited.

'Where are you having it done?' I said. 'They told me it wasn't possible.'

'They do it routinely in America,' she said, 'but here I've only found one surgeon in Salisbury who does it. I'm having it done privately, so he is coming up to Guildford in November to do it for me.'

She showed me a book called *Dr Susan Love's Breast Book*, which showed pictures of the three operations that were possible at the time. There were *three*. Not only the one they had recommended to me at the hospital, but two others.

There was one where the breast was made using the buttock, but that was for very thin women who had no flesh anywhere else, whereas I had plenty of flesh everywhere else.

Then there was the one I had dreamed out of my imagination, which was based on the idea that if they needed to fashion a breast from other parts of me, why not use the parts that were quite definitely going spare? In this operation the breast was made from the abdomen, using the long muscle that runs down the stomach. The blood supply would remain attached, as in the back muscle op, and they would fold the long abdominal muscle over and bring it up to the breast cavity.

I went home from the group and informed Mark that we were moving to Salisbury, to where this surgeon lived, so that I could have my op. He was thrilled to bits. Not.

He begged me not to pursue the more complicated belly-to-breast operation. I assumed his reaction was about not wanting to move to Salisbury. I didn't know at the time that he was terribly squeamish about surgery and any unnecessary choppings-up were anathema to him. But surgery was inevitable if I was going to survive.

The variety of breast reconstructions on offer wasn't the only thing I learned during my first meeting at the support group. The Mavericks believed in turning their attention towards life and away from death. Their message was loud and clear: 'It is possible to survive this, if you eat well and think well. Look at us. We don't just carry the message; we are the message.'

How they cheered me up, making me think for the first time that survival was not only possible but assured.

What a little thing it is, I began to think, in the great scheme of things, to have one's breast removed.

Surely anyone can deal with that?

The Coming of Mr C

I had been involved with about seven medics by the time I got to see the big man himself: Mr C, the oncologist. I was outraged that he had been away on holiday, hang-gliding in the Caribbean or shrieking on the roller-coaster at Butlins (although that was less likely). But wherever he had been, I wanted him home, and quickly.

In my opinion, medics should not be allowed to have lives outside the hospital. They are like teachers, who should sleep in the staff-room or hang upside down in the stationery cupboard until they become useful again at 9am the next day. And like Mums, of course, who are not on any account allowed to be ill. Not even for five minutes.

So I was cross when I walked into his room. But only for a moment. All resentment evaporated the instant I saw Mr C.

He had come. After all these years of waiting, He had returned.

It was Adam Adamant. In the flesh.

'Adam Adamant Lives!'
'In this 1960s television comedy drama, Edwardian adventurer Adam Adamant is frozen alive in a block of ice by his arch-nemesis The Face in 1902. In 1966 workmen discover him and he is revived, perfectly preserved... but completely bewildered by his new environment, 'swinging 60's' London,

until he meets up with the beautiful Georgina Jones, who helps him adapt – and before long, he is back to adventuring, solving crime & fighting evil wherever it may lurk...'
from the Internet Movie Database

My cancer surgeon was the dead spit of Gerald Harper, the actor who played my hero. Adam Adamant himself was going to have the dubious pleasure of lopping off my breast. And who better to do the job than the swashbuckling hero who made it his business to save the lives of any fair maidens he happened to stumble across? I played along with his secret identity, safe in the knowledge that everything was going to be all right now.

It was mad to make a swashbuckling hero of my surgeon. But I just wanted to feel safe, as safe as I had felt sometimes in my Dad's strong arms, those times when he wasn't raging at my Mum.

1957-1969 Horse Play

My Dad wasn't all bad.

Sometimes – perhaps when he had been drinking – he was a cruel and vengeful man. And I was so afraid of him that I screwed down over that fear a veneer of adoration and polished it until I couldn't see through it; until I could only see my own reflection in its surface. And I made sure that the reflection I saw was not of me, but of the person my father wanted to see.

But I also loved him. Children usually love their parents, no matter how badly they are treated. If they didn't, they wouldn't get so screwed up by them.

I remember sitting on his lap. Horsey-horsey bounced the knee; horsey, horsey, horsey, horse. Then suddenly the legs would open and, shrieking, I'd tumble between them to the floor.

Dad

'Let's play horsey-horsey! Dad! Horsey-horsey!'

In the long hot summers, Dad would sometimes come home early and we would cycle to the open-air swimming pool across the town.

And once I was allowed to come with him when he took Pussy to the vet. She was a sweet little tabby called Twinkle, but I always called her 'Pussy'.

I'm sure the RSPCA would be horrified to learn exactly how he took this little cat to the vet, but it was the 1960s then and all sorts of malpractice went unnoticed in those days. Anyway, it was much too far to carry her; he didn't have a car and couldn't afford a taxi. So there was nothing else for it…

Though Pussy didn't like it and made her feelings plain, Dad stuffed her in the duffle bag on the back of his bicycle and we set off. My job was to be lookout, bringing up the rear. I was to keep my eye on the bag and shout whenever it looked like she was getting out.

I watched carefully, not looking at the road and never afraid of being run over, because I was tied by an invisible string to my invincible Dad and that meant that I was safe.

First, two little black eyes would appear and then a nose; then Pussy would push her face through the gap until her ears, squashed back, finally popped out. Said ears would stick up, momentarily, before flattening again with fright against her skull.

As soon as her whole terrified head was sticking out of the duffle bag I would start shouting.

'Dad! Dad! She's getting out!' and as fast as he could, he would stop and squash her back in. I was very important in my role.

In the vet's waiting room, she peed on him. I laughed and laughed as he held her up in the air so that the stream of pee pointed away. But no matter how far away from his body he held her, the yellow stream always managed to find his shoes. Clever Pussy!

Sometimes, Dad would put me up on his shoulders and I would scream, high up on the roof of the world, with nothing between me and the top of the beanstalk and the sky with no end to it and only space to fall upwards into and pain to fall down towards and I would scream, 'Let me down!'

I wanted to feel the ground again so much. How I missed the ground that I had once taken for granted. And down on the ground again, I would clamour to climb back up.

At other times I would dance on his shoes. While I stood on

*his toecaps, he would hold my hands up high and lift his toes –
complete with me – and up, up and round we would waltz, so
slowly, like dancing bears, until he said, 'No more.'*

*'No more,' he would say, too, when we played tigers. I would
ride on him and hit him to make him go and he would roar,
until he tired of it and said 'No more.'*

*Sometimes I ran at him and shouted, 'Hold my hands, quick!
Hold my hands, Dad,' and climbed up the leg and turned right
over into a somersault.*

*And sometimes I would hurl myself down at his feet when
I could catch him standing still. I would sit on one foot and
cling to his lower leg, my arms wound around so tightly; my
legs wrapped round too and crossed at the ankles. Even my feet
would hook together around his leg.*

*Then off he would go – complete with me - dragging his leg
after him like the great wooden leg of Long John Silver.*

Complete with me. And me, complete.

Belt and Braces

Mr C wanted to talk about my treatment. He offered me
chemotherapy and radiotherapy before the operation. He said
that they wouldn't consider giving me radiotherapy after the
operation, so if I was going to have that, I'd better have it now.

It was a once in a lifetime offer and I felt quite pressurised
by the ticking clock. He told me that during the op they
were going to remove lymph nodes from my armpit,
which would be how the cancer would spread if it was
of that mind. He also said that whether or not the cancer

had spread would decide whether or not I actually *needed* chemotherapy, and that they couldn't know *that* until after the operation.

But then he recommended I should have it before the operation in any case.

'So,' I said, slowly, 'if the cancer has spread, then I will end up having chemotherapy before and after the operation?'

'We will make our decision about that when we see the lymph nodes.'

'So,' I said again, 'you're saying that the pre-operative chemotherapy might not be necessary and we won't know that until after the operation.'

'Yes.'

'Well, why would I want to do that?' I said.

'You're not going to have your operation for a few weeks because you want the mastectomy and reconstruction on the same day. And some people in your situation like to feel that they are doing something helpful straight away.'

'What would be helpful about it?'

'It might shrink the lumps.'

If they shrink the lumps, I thought, they're going to be more difficult to find. Idiotic though it may be, that's what I thought. So I politely declined the offer.

'And what about the radiotherapy?' I asked.

'We could do that before the operation but not afterwards,' he repeated.

'Why?' I said.

'We wouldn't want to irradiate the wound,' he said.

I didn't fancy that either and said so. In fact, the whole

package was not particularly lighting any fires with me.

'If you're cutting out all the cancer,' I said, 'why would I have to have chemo anyway?'

'It's the belt and braces effect,' he said. 'All the macroscopic cancer will be removed by the surgery. Macroscopic means the cancer that we can see. And then we come along with the chemotherapy to mop up all the microscopic cancer. That's the cancer that we can't see.'

'But if you can't see it, how do you know it's there?' I said.

'If we found any cancer in the lymph nodes,' he said, 'we would take that as an indication that the cancer is spreading and we would recommend chemotherapy accordingly.'

I pondered this for a few seconds. I didn't fancy chemotherapy. I didn't want to lose my hair and feel sick all the time. I hate feeling sick. And I especially didn't fancy having it when it might be unnecessary.

'No thanks,' I said, 'not before the operation. Maybe after.' Mr C smiled and nodded.

'Let's wait and see,' he said. He seemed pleased that I had made that decision.

I wondered insanely if it was because there was a run on chemotherapy at the moment and they were getting a bit short. Yes, I thought. That'll be it.

Dear Dr A

I met your patient for the first time today having just returned from holiday.

As you know she has multifocal carcinoma in her left breast. The various options have been discussed with her at length and she has done a lot of background reading.

We went through the options again today and she is in favour of pursuing a mastectomy with a view to axillary clearance for full pathological information. She would like to pursue the option of an immediate reconstruction and I have asked my plastic surgeon, Mr D, for his assessment prior to us undertaking a combined procedure. Once we have all the further pathological information we can then decide on her most appropriate adjuvant treatment, although I would agree with my colleagues and other correspondence that it is highly likely that she will need chemotherapy, but I think she needs to be taken one step at a time to explain in detail the indications for her adjuvant treatment.

She has asked me to delay any surgery until the middle of October because of a very important engagement to her in mid October. I am in agreement to this. She will see my colleague Mr D shortly for discussion about the options with regard to reconstruction and no doubt you will hear from him shortly. I will keep you informed as to her progress.

With best wishes
Yours sincerely
Mr C
Consultant Surgeon

Belly-Up

'Once I loved such a shattering physician,
Quite the best looking doctor in the state.
He looked after my physical condition
And his bedside manner was great'
Cole Porter, 'The Physician', 1933

'There's an awful lot of you, isn't there!'

The plastic surgeon smiled sadly. He had hold of my belly. He weighed it in his hands. A pound of flesh. Or two.

'Eh?'

Not two minutes before, when he had come behind the screen and seen me sitting with the towel still wrapped around me, petrified that for the first time in seven years someone other than Mark would see my fat belly, he had seemed to promise me, without speech, that he wouldn't hurt me; that I should trust him and let go my towel.

He shone with virtue. He was the great surgeon, the master-craftsman, who brought beauty to the fallen ones; to the maimed, the horribly scarred and the deformed.

He took a firm grip on the towel and pulled gently. I wouldn't let go.

'No,' I said. 'I don't want you to see it. I can't let you.'

Hitherto in my appointments with the oncologist and all his minions I had obligingly exposed my breasts. I had been poked and prodded, X-rayed, had needles shoved into me everywhere. I had been harpooned, smeared with jelly and shot with an ultrasound gun; I had allowed the students to stare at me, not even knowing, really, what they were looking for. And now this: this stranger was asking me to expose my horrible great big dangly-down belly.

He pulled at the towel and I held fast. He pulled harder. So did I.

He stopped pulling suddenly and held my gaze, his exquisite mouth curving gently; and then he whispered, 'I've seen some terrible things, you know.'

For a moment we stayed there, me perched on the edge of the bed and him standing. Our two pairs of hands locked onto the towel with a *rigor mortis* grip. We stared at each other and his bright blue eyes spoke to me.

'*Is this so important in the great scheme of things?*' they said. '*Is it so awful? Can it possibly be as awful as seeing cancer eating its way across someone's face? Or some hideous congenital deformity? Or terrible burn wounds? I don't think so.*'

'No,' I thought. '*It isn't as awful as that.* '

'*Sssh,*' his eyes seemed to say. '*Don't worry. I won't ever hurt you.*'

I let go of the towel. He touched me gently and curiously all over, as if I was already dead and he was a pathologist. He cupped my breasts and weighed them, checking the droop. Great respect for the dead, he showed.

Then he suddenly took my fat belly in both hands, waggled it and said, 'There's an awful lot of you, isn't there?'

And that's when I died, right there and then, on that pretend operating table.

Then I remembered a story I had heard about a woman with a prolapse, who'd been instructed to jump up and down and pee into a bucket in front of the Consultant and his nurse while she tried to stop the flow. That seemed a lot worse than mere belly-waggling. I came back to life and tuned into what the surgeon was saying.

And it was helpful.

He told me all the worst of it. He said he didn't like the operation where they fold over the transabdominal muscle and keep the blood supply because it can leave the patient with a bulge in the middle of their abdomen. He preferred to cut the muscle out completely and sew the blood vessels together.

'Within two days of the operation,' he said, 'we will know whether or not the blood supply is going to take, and if it doesn't, the tissue will die.'

'What then?' I said.

'Well, we could do the op again, but this time using the muscle from the back, still attached to its own blood supply. Not straight away, though. You'd have to come back after you'd healed because you would have had too much of a trauma.'

'As long as you don't sew it back onto my stomach,' I said, 'I'm easy.'

He told me that because I was so overweight my missing belly would accentuate the fat bits at the sides, and I could see the logic of that. But when I argued that whilst I could lose the weight everywhere else, I would find it virtually impossible to get rid of the fat in my horrible dangling stomach, so it would be great to have it taken away, he agreed that this would be the lesser of two evils.

Also, I thought, I could go back later and have any peculiar tucks and bulges taken off when I was as slim as I wanted to be. And I could wear things that disguised the odd bump. He agreed that I would still look better than I did at the moment, at least belly-wise. He warned that I might have a slight bulge on one side of my abdomen because of the missing long muscle, and I might have to wear a teddy-girdle or something. I don't know where he got 'teddy-girdle' from. I struggled for a second with the image of a teddy-bear bum-bag, tied around my middle, until I realised that he meant a corset.

He warned me about the terrible long scar, right across my stomach. I said, 'Nil desperandum,' which I believe is Latin for 'No sweat'.

I'd seen pictures in magazines of women who'd had tummy tucks and bitterly regretted it because of the scar and the strange position of their belly button, and I'd thought, 'If I looked half as good as that I'd be really happy! They're silly women who thought they would walk out of hospital looking like Pamela Anderson in her prime.'

'And who's going to see my scar anyway,' I thought, 'except Mark, and he, surely, despite all his protestations, doesn't want me to go on looking like this?'

I was determined to use this opportunity to get rid of my fat belly and no amount of warnings or sensible remonstrations would have turned me from my path.

Dear Mr C

Thank you for referring this pleasant lass with the multifocal carcinoma of the left breast, who is for a left mastectomy.

I have gone over reconstructive possibilities with her and she is very keen for a tram flap. I don't like pedical tram flaps and prefer to do a free tram.

If you are happy, perhaps we could do this with you carrying out the mastectomy as usual and then give me a hand as you wish with the reconstruction.

I look forward to discussing this with you.

Best wishes

Mr D

Consultant

How bizarrely we all planned my trip and chose my breast operation. It was almost as if I was going on holiday. I decided that I would use the six weeks before I went into hospital wisely, and prepare myself emotionally and physically for the operation by losing all my excess weight. It shouldn't be difficult, I thought, now I'm motivated.

I wondered if Mark would come on the diet with me. Food was to us what egg is to a beef burger: a binding agent. Messing with that, I knew, would be dangerous to our relationship. But not as dangerous as staying overweight would be to my health.

And the First Rule of Fat Club is?

Me, before I gave up donuts

Mark was a wonderful cook, the kind that could make a delicious meal out of half a tomato and a piece of string. We shared a passion for eating and over the years had grown fat together. He seemed to be ok with being porky, but I wasn't; it made me utterly miserable. I reached my heaviest weight of sixteen stone when I was pregnant with Michael, because I was only free of the nausea when I was eating.

My many attempts at dieting failed, which puzzled me because I'd been a successful dieter when I was young. Then I found a book which argued that diets don't work anyway; that we should adopt the habits of naturally thin people, who eat whatever they want and stop when they've had enough.

With great joy I recruited Mark to this philosophy and we used it to justify a binge-fest that lasted for years; one that rendered us both even fatter. It was the stopping-when-you've-had-enough bit that eluded us.

When Michael was born I walked him every day in the pram and lost my excess weight too quickly, which is how I ended up with my horrible dangling belly. And alas I piled the weight on again when I fell pregnant with Abbie, and this time it didn't shift. I felt as if I was fighting a losing battle.

But now I had cancer, and that changed everything. I had read that diet was a factor in breast cancer and that being overweight was dangerous in operations, so this time I mustered all my resolve, determined to put a stop to my overeating. My friend Julie helpfully roped me into attending the local diet and exercise club.

I liked the aerobics and the diet was excellent; or it would have been if I had stuck to it. In fact, it would have been a fine thing if I'd stuck to any diet.

For a while I went to the class twice a week and puffed up and down the room with everybody else. The pounds fell off Julie but I lost weight more slowly. Then I stopped losing altogether.

The ceremonial weighing exercise at the end of each class became a torture. I'm not sure how helpful it is to be weighed in front of everyone else. The class leader didn't shame us by announcing our weight, of course, but when we went back to our seats the women on either side always asked the same question.

'How much have you lost?' they would say. Every single time. To be honest, I did it myself; I just wanted to find someone who was doing as badly as me. But no one ever was.

The poor girl who ran it really believed in the club. She couldn't understand what was going on with me, especially when she found out how important it was for me to lose the weight.

With each session I dreaded the weigh-in more and more, and I knew she would have to say something about it eventually. The day came.

I stared sadly down at the scales. 'So,' she said. 'Nothing for three weeks.' I hung my head like a naughty schoolgirl. 'Why do you think you're not losing any weight?'

I'd better tell her, I thought. I was worried that my failure might cause her to doubt the diet, and possibly therefore her whole reason for being on the planet.

If she gets really, really depressed and commits suicide over my lack of weight loss, I chided myself, it will be entirely my fault.

I considered. I took the plunge. And I confessed.

'Well,' I said, 'I suppose it could have something to do with the crisps, the chocolates, the cakes and the curries…'

She didn't say anything, just nodded. I think she agreed with me though.

One day, I decided, I am going to start my own club.

T-shirts will be printed and distributed to members. They will say:

FAT CLUB

And then beneath, they'll say:

IF YOU'RE TOO THIN, YOU CAN'T GET IN

I'll put scales at the door and have the weigh-in right at the beginning and if any wannabe members are weighed and found wanting, by which I mean to say that if they weigh *less* than thirteen stone, they will be turned away.

So there.

Knights of Rhythm

I was so afraid of the operation that I became almost convinced that I was going to die. It was strange, waiting six weeks for the day of my death.

Luckily I had a special gig to plan for and work towards, the 'very important engagement' that had caused me to delay the surgery. For once I wasn't the singer-for-hire in someone else's band, or providing the dance music at someone else's party, but had organised my own show at the local theatre, with carefully picked musicians from amongst the many that I knew. I was also taking a risk with the repertoire by venturing forward in time from the 1920s and 30s to the songs of my teens, and asking jazz musicians to play pop songs, because that's the musical mix I wanted to create.

It was a Jazz and 1970s show called 'Janice Day and her Knights of Rhythm'. I was particularly pleased with the title, provided by one of the 'Knights'.

It was probably daft of me not to cancel the booking in

view of the circumstances, but it had already been advertised in the local press, and like most performers I had been indoctrinated with the 'show-must-go-on' mentality from an early age.

I worked hard, learning songs I'd always wanted to sing and never had, while part of me thought this might be my last chance. We got a babysitter in. Suze came with her husband and drove us to the theatre. The trio were all there – a string bass, guitarist and fiddle player – and for once were nice to me. Not that they weren't normally nice to me but on other gigs they tended to behave like musicians, in that blokey way that musicians have of teasing and telling terrible jokes and disappearing to the pub when the bandleader doesn't want them to. This time they were calm and pleasant; they hugged me and did as I asked without demur.

Suze said afterwards that Mark watched my performance with shining eyes, and I was surprised to hear that; and then sad that I was surprised, because it highlighted for me that things were not so good at home. He was a street angel and a house devil, as the saying goes, and very much liked people to think that he adored me, though his behaviour at home was less than affectionate. But I played a part in that too. I had withdrawn from him, fearing his lack of support and how much it would hurt me. And the cancer was like a third person in our marriage. My obsession with survival was drawing me away.

I took risks with the material: the Jazz classic *Bluesette* with the impossible middle eight; Billie Holiday's version of *Body and Soul* which changes key halfway through; Van

Morrison's *Moondance*, his rough gravelly delivery being such a far cry from my little voice; a Pentangling song, in 5/4 time, which was difficult for all of us; *The Sun, the Moon and I* from the Mikado, arranged like the theme tune from Trumpton; Ella Fitzgerald's *Tisket-a-Tasket* which never gets an airing; Joni Mitchell's *Blue*, sung unaccompanied; Joabim's material, sung in the Astrud Gilberto way; jazzed-up Bach, with one melody-line from a fugue, copied from a Swingle Singers album and scat-sung, accompanied only by the double bass player, while we both fought to stay in time and keep in tune with each other all the way through to the end; and then a very sad song, 'At Seventeen' by Janice Ian, that made some people cry.

It was put together and performed with love from me to the audience.

Wanting the musicians to enjoy it too, I gave each member of my trio – my Knights of Rhythm – a spot in which to perform their own experiments with sound. The bass player played a piece with his bow and sang along, just like Slam Stewart himself. The violinist played an antique instrument that was part violin and part trumpet, called a fiddle horn, and the guitarist, normally too shy to sing, sang his own composition. Each to great acclaim.

When it was finally over we took our bows and there was applause, there were encores and there was much love.

It was a free-for-all, a mish-mash; a cornucopia of musical delight. Tarantara! It was my swan-song.

'Now the day is over, night is drawing nigh.
Shadows of the evening steal across the sky.'

The next day, back down to earth as a Surrey housewife, I went into town to buy what women want in hospital: the new make-up bag, the new robe and pyjamas and a pristine toothbrush, just in case the old one should fall out of the make-up bag and shame me.

After traipsing round the town I found myself in a café, needing a very large piece of cake. It turned out to be a Christian café. The owners peddled their religion unashamedly and fell on the news that I was about to have an operation like slavering beasts, squeezing tears of self-pity from me and even getting me to pray with them for my survival, or at the very least a pleasant passage to the pearly gates.

To be fair, they did not have to force these measures on me. They asked me politely if I would like them to pray for me and without any hesitation whatsoever I said 'Yes', because even though the God of my youth seemed to have deserted me, right at that moment praying sounded like an awfully good idea.

1957-1996 Things that Go Bump in the Night

When I was young this was a largely Christian country. And 'Christian' meant, to most people, being nice and well-mannered and going to Church.

I went to a Methodist Sunday school from when I was tiny, encouraged by my Mum, though my Dad was an atheist. Things were cut and dried then: Christians were the goodies, atheists were the baddies. Never let a Mormon into the house. Never speak to the Jehovah's Witnesses. People from other races with other religions lived somewhere north of Berkshire.

And the Spiritualists? Where did they fit in?

Nutters. Along with the vegetarians and the nudists.

Unfortunately for me, my Mum was a Spiritualist, which meant that she was a nutter. And my Dad – the atheist – was a baddy.

Being a Christian myself, I was safe in the arms of the Lord, at least until we fell out during puberty (mine, not God's), when I heard from the girl in the next bed at Bible Club Camp that you couldn't be a Christian if you had sex before marriage. I looked ahead at the long barren years with no kissing or cuddling; no games of True, Dare, Kiss or Promise and no strip poker in the woods. I looked at what Christianity had to offer, with its Bible study and songs with terrible lyrics about Jesus being a cool rock guy underneath it all.

Hmmmm, I thought.

So I shook God by the hand, said, 'No hard feelings, I hope?' and for a while, struck out on my own.

My Mum's stories from the great age of Spiritualism were legendary. She spoke of ectoplasm and trumpets floating around the room, of the famous medium who died of shock when she was interrupted in a trance. And she spoke of healing.

The spirits were all around us, she said, all the time, all-seeing and all-knowing, which was an idea that scared me half to death. I was embarrassed to go to the loo, begging the spirits to wait outside for a minute.

When my siblings had left home and Mum had séances in the house, I was petrified, quaking in my bed upstairs, straining to hear the sounds of any heavy-footed spirits who might let themselves out of the séance to go to the loo and stumble into my room by mistake, searing me through with their scary-eyed stare. Thankfully, none of them ever showed up.

There was no point whatsoever in hiding anything from God, said my Mum, since our physical body was only a house we carried around with us, and as soon as it was gone – when we passed beyond the veil – God and everybody else would be able to see all our hideous sins and misdemeanours in plain sight; so we might as well fess up and live an honest life straight away.

Spirit is Love, she would say, almost as an afterthought. God is the Great White Spirit who sees all and knows all and was once a Red Indian.

I jest. My Mum was not so bad. She didn't force her beliefs on me; she just leaked them out now and then. Not enough to brainwash me, but often enough to put me half in the land of the living and half in the land of the dead. I had to be doubly polite and watchful, since I was permanently aware of the unseen dangers as well as the real ones.

So I grew up afraid of the dark, afraid of empty spaces and sudden noises and of being alone. Afraid of things that fly and crawl. Afraid of what was under the bed and what lurked in the shadows. Afraid of ghoulies and ghosties and things that go bump in the night. Just generally… afraid.

But I did like the idea that the spirits could help us to heal the sick. My Mum took advantage of this gift herself, and when I had banged myself or been beaten within an inch of my life by my brother, she would hold the painful part of me, her hand would grow hot and after a very short time the pain would go away. I came to believe utterly in the power of healing.

My Mum regularly attended healing sessions with her pals. She called it 'going to the healing' and when I was ten I asked to go to the healing too. She took me to a woman's house. Everyone was friendly and very, very old (probably in their forties and fifties).

I had painful knees, which the doctor had called growing pains. It didn't help me to know why they were painful. They hurt and I wanted a cure.

After a while one of the ladies 'went into a trance', which meant that she had tight-shut eyes and talked in a different voice. Then she walked about the room, still with her eyes shut, without falling over anything, though it was crowded with furniture and people. I was very impressed.

I was even more impressed when she took the pain in my knees away, never to return.

She also said that she thought I could be a very successful pianist if I worked hard. This was what my Mum wanted me to do, which meant that I was forced to say 'pshaw and nonsense and fiddle-de-dee' (though I did like playing the piano for the entertainment of the next-door neighbour, who often said she enjoyed hearing me through the wall).

But I was sold on healing. And when I was older and had a poltergeist experience, I became even more convinced that the spirit world was real.

We had left my Dad to move across town to an old council house, my Mum finally finding the courage to get us all away from his tyrannical and abusive behaviour, which was a very brave thing to do in the 1960s.

One day, after a fight with my brother, I was brushing my hair in the mirror in my bedroom and saw the doorknob behind me turn very slowly. I knew it was him, sneaking into my room to do me further mischief. So I crept over to the door and watched the knob turn to its full extent and the door open slowly.

I peered around the ever-widening gap, ready to shout 'boo!' and scare him out of his wits, but it was I who was scared then because there was nobody there. The landing was empty.

I looked back at the knob, thinking I must have imagined it turning. Only inches away from my face now, the door began to close, equally slowly, and the heavy knob turned back into place, though I could see no physical hand holding it on the other side.

Naturally, I decided it was one of those spirits I'd been dreading a visit from all my life, one of my Mum's see-through pals.

After a second of shock I filled my lungs with air and whoever or whatever that invisible creature was I think I must have blasted it to Australia with the bloodcurdling scream I then let rip.

Downstairs, my Mum came clean. She admitted the house was haunted and said my sister Chrissie had seen an old lady on the stairs, a claim that Chrissie now denies. My Mum told me she had a quiet word with the old lady and asked her to leave, on account of how she was frightening the children. This may or may not be true, but I have learned not to listen to other people's stories; only to know what I saw and to believe that.

For a long time in my life I was drawn to Spiritualism and brought my Mum great pleasure by following in her footsteps down that road. But then I discovered the New Age thinking and learned to distinguish between the old style 'Spiritism' of my mother – which concentrates on proving survival after death – and the new style 'Spiritualism', which focuses on how we behave right now, and the idea that we are all treading a spiritual path whether we like it or not, so we might as well knuckle down and learn fast, or we'll be sent back to earth as a spider and get squashed by maniacs like me. Something like that, anyway.

I asked my Mum one day why she still sought proof of survival week after week at her clairvoyant meetings. 'When will you finally believe it?' I said. 'And why are you so desperate to communicate with these spirits anyway? They might be no wiser than the strangers in the bus queue at the end of the road. Haven't you always brought me up not to talk to strangers, in this life or the next?'

She just shook her head with a sad little smile and said she would send me spirit blessings anyway, whether I wanted them or not.

And on 15 October 1996, I did want them. I was happy to accept any kind of blessings, whether they came from Christians or Spiritualists or anyone else. I wasn't fussed. That day, the day before I went into hospital, I would even have accepted a pamphlet from a Jehovah's Witness.

Bye Baby Bunting

The children were leaving.

I thought long and hard about the children and what would be best for them. I decided that I shouldn't inflict on them the sight of their mother bloody, bowed and sick. So I sent them away to my sister Chrissie's house for ten days. Mark agreed with me, as he always did when they were young.

It was the wrong thing to do. Abbie was far too young at three to be separated from me for ten days, and Michael was only five. I wish I hadn't done it, but there it is. In life you walk forward; you hit the wall; you turn right or you turn left. That's all there is to it. Years of therapy and I finally get that. At the time I thought sending the kids away was for the best.

I wrote them two letters each: one to be opened straight after my death, and one to be opened on their eighteenth birthdays (apologising that I had been a rubbish Mum by being absent for most of their lives).

I thought at the eleventh hour that I should have borrowed a camcorder. Alas, too late. Writing would have to do. But what to say? How to explain my sudden untimely demise?

I took the line that only the good die young. The idea appealed to me and I hoped it would to them. So I wrote the children mawkishly sentimental letters, telling them that I was so indispensable to the organisation of the Cosmos that Baby Jesus had whisked me off to do an important job with the Angels.

I almost believed it myself.

When the letters were sealed and stored with the birth certificates and passports, I gave in to melancholy. I felt guilty about sending them away, about being ill, about everything. It seemed to me that I hadn't made much of a good job of being a Mum.

In some ways I had been unorthodox. I was a stay-at-home Mum but not a let's-make-dough-dollies Mum or any kind of a hovering helicopter-Mum. I was more of an oh-my-god-what's-that-lodged-up-your-nose sort of Mum.

When they were tiny I washed them in the kitchen sink. I'd

 sit them on a padded plastic changing mat so they were comfy and then fill the sink up with warm soapy water. The first time around, with Michael, it felt like such a wild thing to do – wilder almost than my wild youth – because I was ignoring the Health Visitor's advice on how to bathe a baby in a baby-bath. And although she was always kind and helpful, in my mind the Health Visitor was as frightening as the child-catcher in Chitty Chitty Bang Bang, because I'd grown up with the idea that if you told anyone outside the family what went on inside, someone would be sure to 'call the Social' and they would come and take you away. That prejudice, though daft, ran deep. So I thought that deliberately ignoring the advice of the Health

Visitor was putting myself in danger of having Michael taken away from me.

I thought they would take him away if the house wasn't spotless; if he wasn't dressed by ten o'clock; if they found out I wasn't using the baby-bath. I certainly thought they would if they found out he'd been into bondage at the age of three, tying himself up to things at every opportunity and not being able to sleep unless I tied his hands behind his back. Thank God he grew out of it. But what did it mean?

When he was a baby, I was torn between wanting to do it my way and thinking I should do it the orthodox way, for safety's sake. It seems silly now to have worried so much. In the end, most people do what comes naturally, and by and large the babies survive. And Mark had no strong feelings on the subject. In fact, Mark deferred to all my parenting decisions when the children were little. We tacitly agreed that he knew even less than I did, though he played with them and made them laugh, which was helpful.

So I let the baby-bath grow mouldy in the garage and bathed the children in the kitchen sink, and as soon as they could stand I stood them up to change their nappies. I thought it was humiliating for them to be laid on their backs with their legs in the air and I didn't want that. I wanted them to be proud, to be able to stand up and look people in the eye and say 'This is me. This is my life. I'll do it my way.'

They were like plants that I had grown from a seed.

When he was only little, Michael asked me once if Daddy had given me a sperm. I was shocked, not knowing where he'd heard of such a thing, but answered honestly.

'That's right. Daddy gave me a sperm and it met my egg and turned into a seed. And the seed grew into you.'

The seed might have been half Mark's, but I was definitely the gardener, though gardening is not a talent of mine. I have never been able to keep a plant alive. I try. I really, really try. I hear that they need water, so I give them gallons of it, because I cannot bear to think that they might be thirsty, and then their leaves turn yellow and they drown. Or I give them plant food, masses of it, because I am a generous hostess, and their little plant bellies burst and their little plant livers become diseased from an overdose of goodness. Or I just forget them, and they die of hunger, thirst and neglect.

Whichever way, they die. They always die. I have accepted that my fingers are as black as my mother's are green, for she is so talented in the garden that she can grow a rose bush from a pebble.

But though I may be guilty of planticide I have had more success with the children. I managed to keep them alive inside me, with just the right amount of food and water, for nine whole months.

When Michael, my first-born, came out – so perfect, round and beautiful; shiny-eyed and sweet-smelling; soft and fine; his little head so fragile on his wobbly neck – I was all undone. My molecules were disintegrated and put back together in a different order; and nothing was ever the same again.

I remember holding my hand over the baby's skull, feeling the life pulse beneath my palm. It was magical. I had a strange premonition that it was always going to be the same; that underneath the angry words and the worry and the despair of parenting that was to come, I would still after all just be holding the baby's fragile little head very, very gently in the palm of my hand.

And there I was, only five years later, writing my letters of resignation. Just in case.

That afternoon my sister and her husband came and drove them away from me. When they had finally disappeared and I was waving at nothing, at the memory of those confused little faces in the back of the car, my legs gave way; I sat down in the middle of the road and wept.

Frankenstein's Assistant

Mark couldn't drive, and anyway he was at work, so my friend Penny drove me into the hospital. Everyone wanted to help and that was fine by me. She stayed a while but eventually had to go.

I didn't want her to leave me with the nurse, who was terrifying. Covered all over in wild black hair, she was bowed and twisted with a dreadful hump, a terrific list to one side and a useless leg that she dragged along the floor behind her, while her knuckles grazed the ground.

No, that's not true and it's also not kind. She looked completely normal, just like all the other nurses. Even if she was a bit hairy. And listing. But she definitely had the personality of Igor, Dr Frankenstein's assistant. Still, who knows? Maybe with her little grandchildren, on Christmas Day, she smiled.

She didn't smile at me when I asked her for a bed. She snarled that there was indeed a bed but that it was full of someone else. So I took myself off and found somewhere to hang about for a while.

As I skulked in the TV Room, it occurred to me that physically, at least, there was something familiar about Igor. She reminded me of a school-friend called Madge. The nickname was short for 'Margaret' and was the result of a thoughtless coupling by her parents of her first name with their family name 'Badge'. The inevitable, sublime result was Madge Badge. It suited her. Like Igor, poor Madge was somewhat cosmetically challenged. And puberty was unkind to her, as it was to all of us.

1968-1975 A Superior Being

Madge was large, lumpish and awkward in the way of many pubescent teenagers, cursed with bad skin and wire-wool hair. She was overly hairy and tombstone-toothed, and what's more her body parts seemed to be peculiarly arranged.

With these obvious physical disadvantages a lesser mortal might have suffered from lack of confidence and perhaps chosen to keep a low profile. But Madge had grown up with the knowledge that she had inherited some rather spectacular genes.

Her father had convinced her that he was, in fact, a Superior Being, and according to him Sir George Bernard Shaw thought so too, having said as much in his regular communions with Madge's Dad at séances held in his home.

I thought he might like to meet my Mum, who was also a Spiritualist.

'My father is not a Spiritualist,' said Madge. 'He is a Superior Being. Haven't you been listening?'

I didn't know much about Superior Beings, but I did know that they lived at Wash Common and we only lived up Pyle Hill, so I decided that she was probably right.

Sadly, the effect of these boasts on Madge's status amongst her peers was not the one for which her father might have wished.

The fact that Madge's Dad was a Superior Being, and kept her out of Religious Education lessons and assembly because he didn't want her head being filled with Christian rubbish, would probably have been sufficient on its own; but on top of that ignominy, Madge was a vegetarian, which in the Sixties was a matter of great ridicule.

And if all that weren't quite enough to put her at the top of the freak scale, Madge's family were practising Naturists as well. Roughly translated, that means that they went on holiday to places where everybody sat about 'in the nuddy'. Now, Madge was no oil painting, as I've said, and the thought of her nudity was painful indeed. Added to this we were assailed by the involuntary picture of her Mum and Dad's nudity too.

It was more than we could bear, and for a while poor Madge became the butt of all our jokes. We tacitly agreed that she ought to be punished for bringing the image of her naked parents into our lives.

We ribbed her unmercifully about being a veggie. When she wasn't looking we sneaked her cheese sandwiches out of her bag and put tiny bits of ham in them. We would tell her after lunch that she had eaten meat, then sit back and enjoy her desperate horror.

One time we stole her clothes after games, so that she had nothing to change into when she came out of the shower. She wandered about in a towel, beseeching us to give her back her clothes, though we denied all knowledge of the prank and left her in the changing rooms. Then we sniggered with joy when she turned up fifteen minutes late for Maths, still in her games kit, and was given a detention.

Every Christmas we teased Madge about her Christmas Dinner of nut cutlets, but this went completely over her head. Nothing we said could diminish her excitement, which was understandable I suppose, since the rest of the year she seemed only to eat cheese.

Not long ago I was entertaining friends for dinner and regaled them with tales of how we tormented Madge at school. I was taken aback by their shocked response. Madge was a good-natured, strangely formed rock. We never thought of her as a victim. She always laughed with us, seemingly glad to be the centre of attention.

'That's bullying,' said my grown-up friend Penny. 'You bullied the poor girl.'

'Bullying?' I said. 'Of course it wasn't bullying. It was only Madge.'

But the thought stayed with me, and the next day I dug out her telephone number from an old Christmas card and rang her up.

'Madge,' I said, without preamble, since we were old friends, 'I wanted to say I'm sorry that we bullied you at school.'

'Did you bully me?' she said. She's as confident a person now as she was then and holds a very high-up position in the education system.

'You know we did,' I said.

'Well, if you did bully me I didn't mind,' she said. 'I just felt sorry for you. I thought you were the ones with the problem. I told myself that you couldn't help it; you were inferior.'

I smiled with relief. Of course she thought that. And that was only to be expected, coming as she did from the loins of a Superior Being.

The Ancient Mariner

Finding myself at last with a bed, I was quietly unpacking when a woman on the other side of the ward beckoned me over.

I was very surprised to see that she was wearing sexy, white, pull-up stockings. I wondered if this was the time or the place for garments such as these. I looked around and realised that everyone was wearing them. Were they all sex slave captives? I asked her what they were for and she explained that the stockings were to reduce the risk of an embolism – a blood clot – wandering around the body.

We exchanged pleasantries and, not surprisingly, got onto the subject of breast surgery. She had had a very unpleasant experience, which was highly confidential, she said, because they were 'going through a legal process'.

I started to feel a little nervous that this story might not be the best one for me to hear right now. There was no stopping her though; and short of screaming for help from Igor, I could do nothing. There was no escape.

Apparently her breast implants had scarcely been put in before they started to degrade. She'd had several operations to put it right, and eventually one had fallen out onto her dinner plate. That was the gist of it, anyway.

I was on my way back to my bed when the soothsayer appeared, as if from nowhere.

She was very, very old. She held me with her skinny hand and told me that I would re-invent myself, and that I would like what I became.

I didn't understand her at the time. After the unholy ministrations of Igor the Transylvanian nurse, and the strange woman across the ward with the irrepressible implants, I was beginning to feel a little surreal.

I snarled at her like a cornered dog (one that could speak): 'Hold off! Unhand me, grey-beard loon!' and followed up swiftly with some more Coleridge to drive my point home. 'I fear thee, ancient Mariner!' I yelled. 'I fear thy skinny hand! And thou art long, and lank, and brown, as is the ribbed sea-sand!' It did the trick. She hissed and scampered away to her bed, unnerved to discover someone who was every bit as bonkers as she was.

Actually, of course, I didn't say any of that.

I merely smiled politely, gently unclasped her hand from my arm and returned to my bed to ponder her words.

What did she mean I would re-invent myself and like what I became? I couldn't imagine. I had breast cancer. I was overweight, about to lose a much-beloved breast and possibly to die.

Meanwhile I continued my unpacking, apparently without a care in the world.

I was putting a brave face on it, but shivered, remembering that apart from when I had Michael (I'd rebelled and given birth to Abbie at home) I hadn't slept in a hospital bed since I was three years old...

1960 All Made of Paper

DATE ADMITTED: 4.10.60
DATE DISCHARGED: 7.10.60
DIAGNOSIS: Unhealthy tonsils and adenoids
TREATMENT: Tonsils guillotined. Adenoids curetted.
SUMMARY:Uneventful recovery.

My Mum and Dad are going. The room is white with rows and rows of beds stretching as far as I can see and they leave through the doors that don't shut properly and I see their faces through the round window that doesn't have proper glass in the doors that kiss but don't shut and I scream and scream and scream,

'Mummy! Daddy!'

Scream louder, they'll come back! Scream louder, they're going! They're going!

But they are gone.

I am abandoned; standing upright on the carpet, turning and turning and turning in that place; looking every which way for the enemies that might appear at any minute; plucking endlessly at the funny paper bracelet on my wrist.

And then they come.

They put a hoover over my face and suck out all my insides through my mouth, so that thereafter and forever more I am made only of paper.

I will have to be careful from now on that I do not rip.

Later I wake up with a sore throat. It's dark.

Nothing to see but rows and rows of beds and the girl in the bed next to mine has taken my doll and says it is hers.

When Mum and Dad come back, as they do after a long, long time, I tell them that I lived in heaven before I was born and I can remember what it was like. It's true. I can remember the ice-cream there.

Years later, Mum says that when I came out I hardly left her alone for the next six months. Apparently I followed her from room to room and clung to her skirts. But Mum says a lot of things...

An Excursion

The plastic surgeon came to my bed and spoke to me. He drew me pictures and explained the whole thing very carefully, but he kept telling me off for asking my butterfly questions.

His diagrams, drawn on a little naked figure on the page, frightened me. I felt overwhelmed and was grateful when a second nurse came and took me to be photographed.

As we travelled the endless quiet corridors, I made a long speech expressing all my confusion about the nature of the NHS. It went something like this:

'You work and pay taxes all your life and don't really think about where the money is going to. Then suddenly all these people descend on you and take over your life and do all these things for you and don't expect anything in return. But you don't make any connection between what's happening and you having paid your taxes and having statutory rights and stuff like that. It's weird.'

Somewhere towards the end of the speech I realised I was drivelling so I stopped and asked her if she knew what I meant.

'Yes. I do,' she said. I was encouraged. So I said, 'Tell me about this NHS thing then.'

'Well, we don't have enough money. And you can't run it like a business.'

She had misunderstood me. I was trying to say, 'Is this care real? I mean, is it real love? Should I be desperately grateful to the nurses and doctors or merely thank them politely but with disinterest, like I would a bus driver? Because right now I want to be loved. I don't want to be meaningless to you. I don't want to be just the Tramflap in Bed Seven.'

By this time, however, we'd reached the photographers unit, deep in the bowels of the hospital, and I was distracted from my thoughts.

I was excited to see that it was a real studio, complete with the silver umbrella that reflects light and a large white background screen. I felt at home there and posed dutifully, half-naked, for the camera.

But as he took photos of me at various angles I started to feel weird again and laughed. It was so ridiculous. Did people come up to him at parties and say 'What do you do for a living?' and did he reply, 'I photograph women's tits'?

'Do you do this all the time?' I asked him.

'Oh yes,' he said, clicking and flashing.

'What a brilliant job,' I said, 'photographing naked women all day.'

'Can't complain,' he said.

And me? I wasn't averse to being photographed. Not then.

Blood, Sweat and Tears

We left the studio and the nurse asked me when I had last had my bloods done. After she had explained the question, I confessed that it had been six weeks and she said I must have it done again. She took me to another waiting area and I asked her to leave me alone because I wanted to have a bit of a wander. Actually it was because I wanted to have a bit of a cry.

The waiting room was like Clarks shoe shop, where the customers have to take a ticket with a number and wait until they are called. I started weeping into my hands.

There were two children who seemed to be there on their own; they stared at me dispassionately. I wanted to stop crying so that I could make the children feel better but I couldn't, even though I knew I should. I crept into the Ladies and sobbed quietly to myself.

It had all become too much. I was overwhelmed with information and feelings that I couldn't identify; but mostly I felt afraid.

I couldn't stop even when they came for me and stuck another needle into me to draw blood.

While I was still crying they patched me up and told me to go back to the ward. I walked back very slowly. I didn't want anyone in the ward to see that I'd been crying. They had all been saying how brave I was and I didn't want to burst their bubble.

It was daft. Actually none of them expected me to be 'brave' and no one in the corridors was surprised that I was crying. Why would they be? This was a place where people were ill, where they had surgery, where they were afraid, where some of them died, where crying was par for the course. But still, I didn't want Igor – especially Igor – to see my weakness.

On my way back to the ward I came across an area that was sheeted off with big strips of plastic. It was partitioning a little courtyard with a bench and some huge plant pots. It was so pretty; an oasis in a desert. I moved one of the strips and breathed the fresh air through the gap. It was pleasantly mild. I gazed longingly at it for a moment, then pushed through the plastic and emerged into the little garden, where I sat on a bench. It felt naughty.

Momentarily, sitting outside in the fresh air, I was escaping, just as I had done so often when I was a child.

1969-1972 Escaping for a While

I was distressed by my parents' divorce. Even though my Dad was a no-good bastard by all accounts, I loved him and didn't want to leave him. And it was traumatic in other ways. We moved from our comfortable 1960s semi with the corner garden that had the miles and miles of woods and fields at the bottom of its road, to a dark, tiny, terraced house on a cramped old council estate. There was only a dual carriageway at the bottom of this road and the nearest park was a ten-minute walk away. Through the park were the canal and the River Kennett. In the triangle of land formed by the apex of those two waterways, where the canal was siphoned off from the river and followed its own path, was my secret place…

No one was ever there, or even seemed to know about it. Of course someone must have owned the land, but at the age of twelve I lived in a simpler world. As far as I knew, that secret garden was all mine.

There was a twisted tree at the river's edge and someone had wedged an old door across a fork of two branches that stretched out over the churning water. I never thought about who might have put the door there. I simply accepted that it was there, and all for my convenience.

I often went there in the evenings and sat cross-legged on the door while I stared into the water; confused, full of hormones, wanting something but not knowing what, dissatisfied with what I had and looking for something else to calm my crazy adolescent spirits. It was a magical place, and precious to me.

Then one Saturday afternoon I shared my secret with Madge, Patsy and Kathy Carter. They shouted and laughed; splashed in the river and chased all the magic away. It wasn't the same after that.

Soon after, someone cut down the hedge, mowed the lawn and put a couple of benches there. And ruined it.

But the night still called to me. While my Mum watched television in the front room, I tiptoed out of the back door and walked to the swings in the big park. Again, I was seeking thrills: the thrill of fear I felt when I walked into the park, and then the aftermath: the peace of swinging in the dark night with only the squirrels for company.

Afterwards I would sneak home to bed, letting myself in the back door quietly. And my Mum never knew – to this day she doesn't know – that night after night, I wandered the dark park on my own when I was only twelve years old.

After a while I hitched up with two young lads, one little

and one large, who were blessed with neither charm nor good looks. What they were blessed with was with a scooter, and they offered me a ride. Naturally I accepted and it became a regular arrangement. When I sneaked out at 10pm they would be waiting for me, eager, I believe, to feel my arms around their waist as they drove me around the estate. Sometimes I would bring my guitar and we would sit on the pavement and sing quietly together so as not to wake up any grown-ups. Our repertoire consisted of one song, 'Bad Moon Rising', which we performed to great mutual satisfaction.

There was talk of a band and a future together, but after a while our friendship began to pall. I don't remember why, exactly. I think maybe one of them had tried to kiss me and I didn't like them in that way. I only liked their scooter and their bad moon rising. I stopped going out to meet them and that was the end of the affair.

I wanted to escape the pressure of my painful feelings. My father and my two sisters were gone. My brother tormented me with his vicious wit and my mother was as crazy and unpredictable as she had always been.

If I couldn't play the piano furiously or sing compulsively, then I had to get out of the house, where the wide sky whisked my feelings up into the air; where I could breathe deeply and relax for a little while.

When we moved from the grotty council estate to the posh new council estate, which was heart-breakingly built upon the open fields of my childhood, I transferred my escaping to the daylight hours and went out in the early morning...

'What have you got in the bag, love?'

The police car had stopped beside me and I was forced to stand still and answer their questions. I wasn't afraid. I was almost glad of the company. I speculated after the event that maybe they thought I was carrying a bomb. Or maybe they were trying to catch me running away from home and were searching the bag for my toothbrush. Looking back, I believe they were just curious.

At the time, I didn't really care. I was happy to show them.

I held the bag up and opened it out. There was an apple and a lump of cheese.

'Where are you going?'

'To see my boyfriend.'

'Well, he's not going to thank you, is he?'

'He might,' I said, feebly.

'It's 5.00am,' said the policeman. We looked at each other. This was an irrefutable fact and – it couldn't be denied – a severe impediment to the credibility of my story.

'Hop in and I'll take you home. You shouldn't be wandering about on your own at this time of the morning.'

It seemed to me that this restriction on my freedom on the basis that I was putting myself in danger was entirely unreasonable. How many mad axe men, I wanted to say, are likely to be out at 5.00am and looking for victims? None at all. There was nothing about, except perhaps the odd milk float and the wind whisking paper litter playfully along the pavements. It felt completely safe to me.

The police stop-and-search attack notwithstanding, I was often up this early, walking the little country lanes, looking for and finding peace of mind in the silence that spanned many miles, the silence of no traffic and no people; no one else's footsteps to disturb me; nothing but the soft breeze, the sharp air and the sound of the birds.

When the dawn was just breaking, I would lie in bed and listen to the birds, and sometimes their call was so insistent that I would get up and go out to them, especially when the day was clearly going to be very hot.

Most of my journeys had no purpose, but a few times I went to fetch Patsy for a walk or braved discovery by the police again to cross town and wake up Sean, my first proper boyfriend, to get into bed with him, to kiss and cuddle.

I would wake both these great loves of my life by throwing stones at their bedroom window.

Patsy thought it was tremendous at first but then began to refuse me. 'I'm sleepy,' she would cry, but I wouldn't let her alone. I wanted to go for a walk with her and there was no escape.

The first time I did it to Sean he was thrilled and couldn't stop giggling. The second time, he was cross. And going to Sean's was difficult. I had to walk across town. The police picked me up twice and took me home to my Mum, who wisely didn't make a fuss, confident that I would grow out of the behaviour. And of course I did.

Reluctantly I came back to the present again and shivered. The night was drawing in and it was getting cold. The haven I had imagined this little garden to be was an illusion: I suddenly saw that it was scruffy; the plants were dying and there were windows all around the courtyard. I no longer felt that I had escaped. Patients' rooms overlooked me; people could be watching. I was even more exposed here than I had been on the ward.

It was a defining moment.

I realised that there was no escape at all, not from any of this. No cellars or attics to hide in. No play swords to fight with. No school pals to rescue me. No point in playing truant. The only way forward was through. I accepted the place I was in, and for once stood still.

I slept well that night; and the next morning I woke up bright and early and ready to be chopped up.

Going Down?

It was the day of the op. I had a bath so as not to be offensive to the surgical team and when it was nearly time to go I received an unexpected phone call from Lou, my friend in Hong Kong.

'I wanted to wish you luck with the operation,' she said. I was thrilled. It meant so much to me that she had bothered. The simple act of kindness cheered me up no end, and if it's true about the power of positive thinking, mayhap it even saved my life. Who knows? Suffice to say that I was almost perky when the porter came to take me down to surgery because I knew that I was loved.

I asked if I could take my bear. One of the nurses put a surgical hat on the teddy's head, which made him look official. I was thirty-nine, but there are times in life when a bear is important and this was one of them.

Igor wasn't there, thank goodness. She was busy, probably sucking the life-blood from a young virgin.

And we were off. The magnolia ceiling rushed by above my head as I flew backwards down the corridors and soon – too soon – we were in surgery, and they were asking me to count backwards from ten… backwards into oblivion and earlier… earlier still…

1961 Doctors and Nurses

Fat Bea's naked body quivered and wobbled where she lay on the floor in Andy Jones's loft. We gazed in awe at the vast expanse of her white marbled flesh, marvelling at the gently rolling contours, fascinated by mounds and folds that neither of us could see on our own skinny young bodies.

Andy Jones was still fully clothed. Fat Bea and I had flatly refused his offer to be the Patient and he had to be content with the role of Doctor. It had its advantages: it gave him charge of the Doctor's Bag and what's more, the Straw.

'Okay,' he said, 'The Doctor has the Straw.' He waved it in the air. 'Now. Who's the patient?'

'Me,' said Fat Bea, hopefully.

'Me!' I said. 'You've just had a turn.'

She rolled onto her knees and crawled out of the way and I was glad. I hadn't liked touching her winkle with the straw. It felt yucky, like the time when some local children had packed my knickers with gravel and then sent me home to my mother, who had smacked me and called me disgusting.

Fat Bea's mother had done the same a couple of years earlier, finding Bea and me not, as she had thought, playing nicely in the paddling pool, but treading wet grass into her long pile bedroom carpet whilst we raided her jewellery box. I was thrilled at the sight of all the shinies and sparklies that we so carefully laid out on the bed. I'd never seen such beautiful things.

I don't think either of us noticed that we were naked. Even if we had, it wouldn't have occurred to us that there was anything naughty about that; but Bea's mother, a devout Catholic, thought otherwise. Like a giant ogress, she burst into the room.

'What are you doing in my bedroom?' she bellowed. 'You wicked children! Put some clothes on at once! You're disgusting!'

In her seven league boots she came, roaring and smacking our bare bottoms. 'Look at that carpet!'

Smack! Smack! One each.

Fat Bea's Mum was ugly and I was frightened. The enchanted castle, stripped of its magic, transformed into a dull, shabby 1960s bedroom. Through her eyes we saw for the first time the muddy grass, the stolen jewellery and our own shameful nakedness.

Didn't Adam and Eve feel like that? Naked and ashamed?

Never mind. Bea's mother wasn't there that day in Andy Jones's loft and nor were his parents. Our nakedness might well have been wicked. But it was all ours. We had delicious secrecy. We had each other. And we had the Straw.

I tore off my nurse's uniform and lay down on the old mattress.

'What seems to be the trouble, Miss?' Andy Jones said, as he and Fat Bea leaned over me.

'I don't know,' I whispered guiltily, since I knew there was none.

'I think you'd better examine her, doctor,' said Fat Bea. 'She doesn't look well.'

'Very well, nurse. Stand aside.'

I closed my eyes, the better to anticipate the coming of the Straw. And then it began. Slowly, slowly and tickling all the while, it traced its delicious path down my body, until it found its way to the secret naughty place between my legs that felt so nice. I held my breath and slid into the sensation, like a bather sliding serenely under the surface of the sea.

Coming round

When I woke again, some nine hours later, it was all over. I was thirty-nine years old again and coming round from a nasty, long op.

Mark was sitting in the corner of my private room, just as he'd been sitting in the corner of a different room when I was in labour with Abbie, sitting quietly and reading. He was grinning at me. I didn't want Mark, though. I wanted someone I hadn't thought about in years.

I had lost my breast, something that was so acutely part of me that the loss of it triggered my earliest memory of loss: the time when I lost Lisa, my first and very-best-best-friend.

1964 Lisa

We may live in a multicultural society now, but I didn't grow up in one. The people in Berkshire were either 'County' – white and predominantly middle-class, farmers and the landed gentry – or they were like us, the lower middle class. The two groups had little to do with each other.

In the first eighteen years of my life I never knew an Asian or a Jewish person and came across only three black girls.

Two of them attended the grammar school. One looked like Jimi Hendrix and was expelled for throwing a chair at a teacher. The other was terribly good; quiet and industrious, and wouldn't have dreamt of having anything to do with me, the naughtiest girl in the school.

The third I had already met when I was five, and for two years she was my greatest love. Her name was Lisa. She lived across the grassy roundabout and a little way up the hill. Lisa was a black American and her parents had something to do with the Airbase at Greenham.

We were inseparable. She was either older than me or very much more self-possessed. However it happened, Lisa took over the care of my life and told me what to do.

She had a shining brown face and magic hair. It was magic because when she plaited it, she didn't need to tie it up with a ribbon or even an elastic band. She would plait it right to the ends and it never unravelled.

We tried and tried to make my hair do the same but it wouldn't, not ever. It was useless, my hair. As soon as the plait was finished and the hands were lifted away, it would start to unravel, unwinding faster and faster. How I cursed it, to Lisa's great satisfaction, with her magic, black, stay-in-place locks.

Lisa and I had one outfit that was almost identical. Some days, when we were going home for our tea, Lisa would make me promise to wear 'our clothes' the next day.

The outfit was so pretty. There was the same bell-shaped dirndl skirt with elasticated waistband, only mine was green-patterned and Lisa's was blue. That was OK; there was room

118

for a tiny bit of individuality in our lives. But the rest of it was the same. We both had shiny black patent-leather sandals with an identical pattern of holes. We both had sleeveless white blouses with a magic hidden button line. The buttons were under a flap. Only we knew that they were there, and it was our shared secret. The ensemble was completed with short white fold-over socks.

One day my mother laid out the long white socks for me, and wouldn't listen when I told her that the socks had to be short. She said it didn't matter; she only had long white socks because all the short ones were dirty.

I screamed and screamed until I was purple. I thought I would die of misery. It didn't matter that she smacked me and shouted at me and dragged me about; I didn't care about living. I only knew that I couldn't go out in those long white socks. Lisa would be wearing short white socks and I must do the same, at all costs, I must do the same.

When I had calmed down a little and was only sobbing quietly in the bedroom, my Mum came and sat by me and asked me why it was so important. I was able to tell her about the outfit then, and the task that had been given me: to wear the outfit. My Mum came good. She fetched the dirty short white socks from the laundry bin and I put them on. Everything was ok again; God was in His heaven, and all was right with the world.

Lisa taught me everything that was important; skills that have carried me throughout my life. She taught me to blow bubble-gum bubbles. She taught me to whistle. And she taught me to belch at will.

Lisa and I thought we were twins. We were so alike apart

from my stupid hair. Lisa was very good about that and didn't make me feel stupid. Everything else about us was the same. We barely registered that we had different colour skin.

But my mother did. My mother didn't like it when I stayed to tea at Lisa's house and came home with a huge bag of popcorn; something we never saw in our house.

She didn't like it that I abandoned my knife and started eating my tea with one upturned fork. I told her that Lisa's parents ate like that so it must be OK.

She didn't like it that I started blowing pink, sticky, chewing-gum bubbles all the time, and that I could whistle and belch at will.

My Mum told me that it would be better if I didn't see so much of Lisa.

'Why?' I asked.

'They're different to us. It's better to keep away from them.'

'Why?'

'Well… they're coloured people.'

I didn't know what she meant. I only knew that something was spoiled. My Mum knew everything there was to know about the world, and if she said that I shouldn't play with someone, I listened to her.

I had thought that Lisa and her parents were wondrous beings, but she thought they were something bad.

And wasn't my Mum there to protect me from everything bad?

Things were not the same between Lisa and me after that. Lisa had been a shining sun-goddess to me but now she was a tainted thing, someone to be avoided because her family were *in some way less than ours. We drifted apart and lost touch altogether over the next few weeks.*

Then one day, when I was colouring at our scruffy old table covered with its green chenille cloth, I heard a knock at the kitchen door.

'Someone's here to see you, Janny,' announced my Mum, awkwardly. 'She's come to say goodbye.'

Lisa stood shyly in front of me. She said her family were going back to America. I was so shocked that my insides froze. I couldn't begin to absorb the pain of what it would mean not to have Lisa in my world ever again.

But I wanted to please my Mum and she was standing beside Lisa looking right at me. I knew my Mum didn't want me to be friends with her so I went back to my work and didn't look up. I only grunted and went on with my colouring.

'Say goodbye,' my Mum said, sharply.

'Bye,' I said, and didn't look up from my colouring. I went on colouring as if it was the most important thing in the world.

'Janice,' my Mum snapped.

'I'm colouring,' I said. I went on, and the silence stretched out from my colouring pencils into the room. Scritch scratch went my pencils. When I looked up, finally, Lisa was gone, and I never saw her again.

My Mum told me off for being rude. I couldn't understand why she wasn't pleased that I had been rude to the girl she didn't want me to play with, the girl whose family weren't 'like us'. I had only done it to please her.

Never mind that my heart was broken.

Being Struck Off

I came in and out of consciousness over the next four hours and every time I opened my eyes Mark was there, grinning in the corner like some ghastly Buddha.

I thought there must be something wrong with him. Even in my groggy state I was concerned that he needed psychiatric help. Why else would he sit there grinning for four whole hours when his wife had just had one of her breasts lopped off?

He later claimed that he could see every time I was surfacing and had arranged a smile on his face in readiness.

But it was unnerving, this constant jollity.

Occasional glimpses of Igor were also unnerving. Once, just as I was dropping off again, I focused briefly on the horrible fat legs wobbling beneath her blue nurse's dress. I couldn't help thinking that if I had legs like that I might not cling to life so fiercely.

'Oh God, I'll be struck off,' I groaned.

'What?' asked grinning Mark. I didn't answer. I was talking to God. And God replied, just as I sank again into unconsciousness.

'Struck off what?'

'The Register.'

'What Register?'

'Of good people. The Register of good people.'

'No you won't,' said God. 'Trust me. I have influence.'

Then, wanting to make absolutely sure that He knew the whole picture and wouldn't suddenly change his mind, I stood in my dreams at the pearly gates and asked for crimes other than the stealing of the Slinky toy in 1967 to be taken into consideration.

Time to Confess

First up in my dream confession was another theft: a washing line from Woolies that me and Patsy Parkin had stolen in the days before the Slinky episode had ended my career in organised crime. It wasn't the slickest of heists. The line was surprisingly heavy, so heavy in fact that we quarrelled constantly about who should carry it, until in the end Patsy put it down on the pavement and stalked off while I scurried after her. I have forgotten why we thought we needed a washing line, but it was probably meant for tying small boys to lamp-posts.

Small boys led me on to confession number two. These creatures were ubiquitous in our childhood, and I invented a brilliant game where we tied one to a lamp-post and left him to perform a feat of daring escapology on his own. This he usually did with no harm done. But one time we forgot about a particular small boy, whose grasp of escapology fell short of Houdini's, and went home for our tea, leaving him supperless until the search party found him drooping wearily from his bonds in the late evening.

My third and final confession, as I stood in my dream at the pearly gates, was a heinous crime indeed and resulted in the breaking of limbs. For the lamp post game we could theoretically have used a larger boy, but for the flying-through-the-air game only a boy of limited mass would do the trick. This involved an older child (me or Patsy) lying on her back with her legs drawn up at the knees. The small boy would then sit on her upturned feet and be catapulted into the sky when she suddenly straightened her legs.

It was an excellent game, but the grown-ups may well have been right when they suggested, as the ambulance screeched off in the direction of the hospital, that something soft to land on might have been a good idea.

All my crimes confessed, I now trusted that God would make good His promise not to strike me off the Register of good people, and really did have enough influence to get me into Heaven. And with that idea, I slept in peace.

The Birth of the Breast

As Mr D favoured a free flap over a pedical flap, my new breast, fashioned as it was from the abdominal muscle and fat from my stomach, did not have its own blood supply. Sometimes the surgeon will not detach the long abdominal muscle from its blood supply, instead folding it over and pulling it up into the breast cavity to form the breast. But in my case the abdominal muscle was detached completely at both ends, with an artery from my groin dangling loose. I thought they would then have to roll it up or tie it in several knots or something to make breast-shaped. Otherwise wouldn't it stay long and thin like a piece of elastic? But no, they told me, the detached muscle shrinks up like a lump of meat

So anyway… the loose artery needed to be plumbed into the artery that was already running through my armpit. The surgeon cleverly put a little nick in it and then sewed the new artery in to form a 'T'. This was the pivot on which the success of the operation balanced. The question was: would the body cooperate and accept the new breast, or not? To give it the best chance, they had to keep me as still as possible for the first twenty-four hours, and in bed for the next.

It was not pleasant. I was in pain: hot, thirsty and groggy with morphine. Never have twenty-four hours felt so long. A team came and checked me on the hour, every hour. Before he left I asked Mark to cut open my nightie so that they could peak in at the breast, feel its temperature and check its colour. He did so and the medics were pleased. After all, what price a nightie, compared to the birth of a breast?

Every hour they came and, satisfied, marched away again. It was happening. Oxygen-carrying blood started to pump around my breast. Tiny capillaries burrowed into the surrounding flesh until every part of the breast was fed with life-giving blood. What a fantastic thing!

Later, I asked the Consultant what would have happened if the blood supply had not 'taken'.

'The breast would have died,' he said.

'Died?'

'It would have gone grey and eventually fallen off,' he said.

'And then what?'

'We would have had to start again.'

'Put the whole thing in the bin and start again?'

'Yes.'

'Good thing it did "take" then.'

'Yes,' he said, 'it was.'

And I believe he meant it, after all his hard work.

Today's Special Offer

When I was lying in my hospital bed, bruised and broken on the wheel of life and with drains sticking out of every orifice (or so it felt), and the 'Plastics Team' floating in and out from time to time with their clipboards and their cheery smiles, someone came and talked to me about nipples.

'These can be made from the vulva or the anus,' he explained.

I responded immediately and with conviction.

Firstly, at that point in my life I needed another painful operation like a hole in the head. And just to make it absolutely clear, because you need to be careful in hospitals, I didn't need a hole in the head either.

Secondly, I particularly didn't need to feel pain in the region of my vulva or my anus, thank you very much.

And thirdly, the thought of walking about with a bit of my arse stuck on my chest was not exactly appealing.

Of course I didn't say any of that. I said, 'Thanks, but I think I'll pass.'

'Are you the Toilet?'

I woke up one of the mornings convinced that I was in a Victorian insane asylum. It was 3am. My room was stark and bare, my bandaging made me feel like I was tied to the bed, and I could hear what sounded like the howling of lunatics out on the ward.

Coming to full consciousness didn't help either. I knew intellectually that I was in hospital following an operation but my body thought I'd been run over by a truck. After a little while I decided to get up and go to the loo for the first time.

They had stuck drains in me: one to pump fluid into somewhere, one to remove urine and two others that did something else, I cannot imagine what.

So that made four altogether, each with a bottle at the end. Feeling like a B-movie sci-fi monster, I gathered up all my bottles and wires so that they would neither pull on my flesh nor knock anybody out.

I could easily have taken out two or three patients by padding across to the ward, letting go of my bottles and performing the dance of the whirling dervish. But I didn't feel much like doing that.

Instead I stood in the door of my room trying to work out how to get my robe on with only one useful arm and all the drains sticking out of me.

A little old man shuffled up to me and said, 'Are you the toilet?' He looked at me expectantly. It wasn't that he mistook my room for a toilet. He actually thought that I was one. I tried to make the sound of a cistern flushing but couldn't do it. I just didn't have the plumbing.

I got back into bed, deciding to write about it because I didn't want to go back to sleep. If I went back to sleep I might wake up feeling like that again and I didn't want to go through it twice.

I called Igor in to ask her for a pen and she was cross because she had been in the middle of a tracheotomy.

Of course she was; I should have known it. She was busy saving someone's life by punching a hole in their throat to allow a passage of air into their lungs, and I only wanted a pen.

In my confused state I berated myself: how could she spare a pen for me when she had just used it to do the tracheotomy, NHS resources not being what they once were…?

Putting on a Brave Face

I kept my brave face in the drawer by my bed. It consisted of foundation, eye-shadow, lipstick and mascara. The nurses couldn't believe that within two days of the operation I was sitting up in bed in full make-up. But that is the performer's mentality: the show must go on. I couldn't let down my fans.

Of course there were no fans. But there were friends and they came… and came… and came.

We had devised a perfect plan to organise the visitors' rota. Aspiring visitors phoned Mark and he wrote their names in the chart I had designed and left for him before I came in. Mark broke the habit of a lifetime by answering the phone to well-wishers and dutifully told my friends when they could come and see me.

The rota was a brilliant conception and was intended to leave me with lots of space for rest and recuperation. It didn't work though. The friends came on time and according to the plan, but our master schedule didn't tell them how long they could stay. So they came and they didn't leave, and the nurses didn't throw them out. So it became like the how-many-people-can-you-squash-into-a-Mini game and the visits sometimes stretched to an hour at a time.

How I longed for the peace and quiet of Igor's neglect and the strangely reassuring moans and groans that wafted through the otherwise silent ward in the blessed night.

It was tough, being popular.

So there I was: a lipsticked and face-powdered starlet in my little private room, with the constant stream of visitors plaguing me with their presents and their merry faces. And their flowers.

The flower-bunch tally reached thirteen. I complained bitterly about them, demanding that the nurses remove them from my room each night. With less-than-total scientific justification, I insisted that flowers are well known oxygen thieves. I don't want to go through all of this, I said, being chopped up into little pieces, rearranged and roughly sewn together again with hemp, just to be bumped off by a bunch of flowers.

I can't be sure – the mind plays tricks – but I think there is a remote possibility that I was a pain in the arse.

Never mind. My friends were grateful to me for being overly made-up and entertaining. Several confided to me in shocked whispers that as they walked slowly up the plastics ward, glancing from left to right, they had seen some terrifying sights. The plastics ward was a veritable horror movie, it's undeniable.

One friend reported that his heart sank further and further into his squeaking shoes as he approached my little room, fearing what he was coming to; fearing especially, I suspect, that his merry face might slip. But it was OK. When my visitors discovered me sitting up and smiling amongst my flowers, all made-up and pretty in my midnight-blue silk gown, they admitted to being quite pleasantly surprised.

'You look like Elizabeth Taylor,' said one, and I chose to believe her.

Eventually I found a way to thin them out. When the conversation flagged, I offered each the opportunity to look down the front of my nightie. There were no takers. They mostly paled and said they had a taxi waiting.

And I was left in peace again.

The Excursion, Reprised

Before the medics let me leave the hospital they took me on a little trip in the wheelchair. I couldn't walk very far without it. Apart from being pulled over to one side by the staples in my stomach, I couldn't seem to get my legs to work. I shuffled everywhere like a little old lady.

'Where are we going?' I asked.

'To the photographer,' said the nurse, 'to have the "after" photos done.'

A date, I thought to myself. As if. They have turned me into a hideous, malformed hag. Maybe there will be no more dates ever, now that I look like the Bride of Frankenstein.

Oh well, I sighed, I've had a good run.

1963 First Love

My first ever object of desire was John Smith. Or little Johnny Smith, depending on your viewpoint. And your height.

John Smith was a romantic figure, albeit a somewhat scrawny and undernourished one. But the six-year-old me adored him, and it was the biggest thrill of my young life when he followed me into the girls' toilets one day with a view to... what, exactly? I didn't know, but I was expecting something dark, dangerous, forbidden... and delicious.

He didn't do it, whatever it was, though I trembled complicitly before him.

I thought he might try to kiss me, maybe offer me a penny to look in my knickers. I had heard of such terrible goings-on.

Alas, he didn't. He merely menaced me briefly in a small boy sort of way, then kicked open one of the cubicles and snooped into a toilet before hightailing back to his gang.

So that was the end of the affair. A damp squib.

But Johnny Smith wasn't my first love. That was Lisa, my best friend when I was five, from whom I was forever parted by my mother's racism.

And after Lisa there was Patsy Parkin...

From the very first minute I saw her, I loved her. We were both out of class, sent out on a task by our respective teachers. I saw her at the top of the corridor and she turned her head towards me. We hung there for what seemed an age, our gaze and little bodies locked into the moment. It was like looking in a mirror.

Sometimes I see someone for the first time and for some reason I know that they are going to be significant in my life. The excitement of the moment seizes me and freezes me in that space, so that there seems to be nothing between me and the other person.

Patsy was the first of those people. We were six years old and frozen at the sight of each other in the dark low-ceilinged corridor at the top of the worn oak steps.

We were both skinny, both had regular picture-book style features, and both had long, silky, red hair. We felt that we were looking at our own reflection.

But there were differences.

Her outfit was a black pinafore over tartan-patterned tights. She looked cool – or whatever that word was in 1963 – whereas I was wearing a bright yellow cardigan with bobbles, and a green kilt into which I was supposed to grow.

What's more, her ponytail was higher, longer, silkier and redder than mine, which was thinner and a more carroty shade of red. Her hair was a rich auburn colour and she was slender like Twiggy. She looked like a young colt. I, on the other hand, looked like a kid, and I don't mean an American child. I mean a small goat.

Not completely the same then, but nearly: we were nearly the same, but she was better. Even then – and ever since – it has been my quest to find someone who loves themselves, and to become them as nearly as I can: by buying all the same things as them; by having their opinions and thinking the thoughts that I imagine they are thinking; and, if the love object is a man, by giving myself physically and so completely that I create the sensation that we are melting together. Thus I can thaw out for a little while, squeezing closer and closer to their warmth, until finally they feel engulfed and struggle to break free.

Some people call this love addiction. Some people call it attachment hunger. Some people call it being a pain in the neck.

Whatever it's called, Patsy was one of those people I wanted to absorb.

For six years following that fateful moment in the dingy corridor, Patsy Parkin was my puppet-master. She was the

criminal mastermind behind my exploits as the naughtiest girl
in the primary and then the grammar school, though she rarely
got into trouble herself.

Only the headmistress guessed this, wise old crone that she
was at the desperate age of forty.

'Patsy Parkin makes the arrows,' she once said to my mother,
'and your Janice fires them.'

There was no sign of Patsy or Mark or anyone I loved in this
lonely corridor outside the photographer's studio, and despite
my best efforts to keep up my brave face, the tears began to
drip and then came fast. Passing patients and staff politely
ignored my distress, which was good, and I was able to stop
after a while.

I was crying because I remembered being there only a few
days before and standing straight with my beautiful proud
breasts on display. And here I was again, painfully aware that
my unkind thoughts about Igor could far more accurately be
applied to myself now. Or not, actually, for she was merely the
doctor's cosmetically challenged assistant, whereas I was the
monster himself, a roughly sewn and bloody patchwork quilt
of body parts.

But the photographer was gentle with me and refrained
from making any jokes along those lines, for which I was
grateful.

It occurred to me that maybe his job wasn't so great
after all.

Everything That Can Go Wrong, Will Go Wrong

I went into hospital on Wednesday. I lost my breast on Thursday, was mistaken for a toilet on Friday, had my drains out on Saturday, was nearly murdered by flowers on Sunday, and was discharged on Monday.

With an infection.

While I was still in hospital they had removed my drains and let me take myself to the toilet, where I noticed that my wee was smelly. That had never happened to me before, so I didn't realise that it signified a urine infection: apparently not an uncommon occurrence after 'wearing' a catheter (the contraption that drained urine from my bladder when I wasn't looking).

My nurse-friend Penny said that I should have been checked for a urine infection. She said it ought to be routine when a catheter has been in place for more than two days. But I wasn't checked. Even when I'd plucked up the courage to mention my personal problem to one of the hospital nurses, she'd just smiled and told me not to worry.

So I came home looking like a pig's ear, not able to stand up properly because of the staples in my tummy and with smelly wee to boot.

I was also in pain; the pain of a thousand paper cuts, and the painkillers from the hospital didn't go anywhere near dealing with the problem. I discovered a very strong painkiller, which seemed to work, not realising that the extra kick in the drug was largely caffeine. I can't drink caffeine because it turns me into an axe-murderer, which might explain why I was raging in the first few weeks and throwing large items of furniture around the flat: quite a feat for someone in my condition.

One furniture-hurling session occurred because I had asked Mark if he'd remembered to insure the house, which I had been on at him to do for ages.

He laughed at me, saying that I surely had more things to worry about than that. I raged back at him with hysterical sobs that I just wanted some small part of my life to feel safe and normal and like everybody else's. To punctuate my words I threw the heavy bedside lamp at his head, which can't have done my wounds any good. Luckily, I missed. But I think he got the point.

Was my rage at Mark inspired by his inability to meet my emotional or physical needs, which were so vast at this time that they were impossible to meet, or just to do with the caffeine? Who can tell? I would probably have been raging anyway. I couldn't sit up comfortably or lie down on my back, or on either of my sides. I couldn't breathe, I couldn't sleep and the breast hurt. It hurt all the time.

Only two things gave me pleasure. The first was the fact that before I went into hospital a group of old friends had banded together and decorated our flat, which had looked like the inside of a bin bag before they started and afterwards was calm and clean and beautiful.

The second was hot water. I stayed in the shower for ages, up to forty-five minutes at a time, revolving endlessly, so that the hot water sprayed my poor bruised body evenly. I kept going back to the shower whenever I could.

Mark eventually banged on the door and shouted for me to come out. 'You'll stop it healing!' he yelled.

'This is the only thing that makes me feel like a human being and not just a mass of screaming nerve endings!' I screamed back. 'I'm not going to give it up!' He couldn't hear me.

Certain that it couldn't be right for me to be constantly wet, Mark made me phone the Plastics Ward and ask permission to have a shower in my own house. Of course they didn't give it.

'No,' said the ward nurse. 'Don't keep having showers. You won't heal if you do.'

I put down the phone and wept. Even now, I cursed, they are still messing with me and ruining my life, taking away my lovely hot showers.

I was behaving like a three-year-old. But at least, so far, I was alive.

29 October 1996

Dear Dr A

This lady had a left mastectomy and free tram breast reconstruction 12 days ago. Despite a UTI, which is currently being treated, she has done well. Her wounds have healed and although she has two hard and tender areas in and around the flap, which are probably due to haematomas, these should settle down with gentle massage. Her steristrips and clips were removed today.

We plan to see her again in about six weeks' time and will keep you informed of her progress.

Yours sincerely

Dr J,

Registrar in Plastic Surgery.

Return to Alcatraz

I didn't think I was getting better. The pain was lessening but I was beginning to feel spacey and remote. I had gone to the doctor about my smelly wee and been prescribed antibiotics; but my resistance was low and I was open to infection of another kind.

One day I woke up with a pretty blush on my new breast. I remembered that they had said to look out for redness, so I rang them.

'How do you feel?' said the nurse.

'Ok,' I said. 'Maybe a bit hot.'

'Come in straightaway,' she said.

'Come in! All the way to Roehampton?'

'Straightaway,' she said.

What a to-do. I didn't want to go back there. I hadn't thought I would ever have to go back to that place where they had chopped me up and rearranged me and spat me out into Igor's tender care.

I asked Penny my nurse-friend to drive me in because I still wasn't supposed to drive. I felt odd in the car, as if I was floating. But it was a quiet oddness, not aggressive like the raging pain of the past couple of weeks. It wasn't unpleasant. I didn't see why I had to go in.

When I got to the ward a nurse had a look at me and drew around my blush with a biro. I thought it was a peculiar thing to do and asked her why she'd done it.

'So we can see where it is,' she said. I was not satisfied with that answer: anyone could see perfectly well where it was. It was pink. Everything was starting to feel a little surreal by that time. But when she returned in five minutes with a doctor and he looked at it, I suddenly understood. The blush was now outside the biro mark.

'What's happening?' I asked.

'You have an infected haematoma,' he said.

I knew this term. This was one of things that the surgeon had told me could possibly go wrong. As it happened, everything that he said could go wrong, did go wrong. I did end up with a surgical hernia; I did have fat necrosis, which means that hard lumps of fat formed inside the new breast and took several years to disperse; I did have thick keloid scars that still haven't quite faded. But this came first. The most dangerous. A blood-clot in the new breast. And infected too.

Blood-poisoning.

People die of that.

'We're going to put you on an antibiotic drip overnight, pump masses of very strong antibiotics straight into your bloodstream and see what happens,' he said.

'Overnight!' I was aghast. He laughed at me.

'This is very serious,' he said. 'We must keep you here for observation.'

They found me a bed. If I hadn't felt so ill I would have cried. Never had I been so miserable. To have escaped Alcatraz, believing myself to be free, back in my own newly-decorated home with the lovely hot showers, back in the bosom of my family… and then to find myself suddenly incarcerated again in the place of death not two weeks later! This was misery indeed.

But it had to be done. They pumped the antibiotics into me overnight, and apparently saved my life.

'Good thing you noticed and came in when you did,' they said. 'It was probably the urine infection that did it. Lowered your resistance.'

But I hardly cared. I protested so much about being there that they let me go. 'Ungrateful wench,' they probably thought. I was discharged the next day clutching three packets of very strong antibiotics that made me feel even more ill than the infection had.

5 November 1996

Dear Dr A

Janice was admitted over the weekend with an episode of cellulitis on the reconstructed breast. This is settling well and I have advised her to finish the course of antibiotics.

I will see her again in five weeks' time.

Kind regards

Yours sincerely

Mr D

Consultant

The Verdict

During my operation they removed thirteen of my lymph nodes and sent them for analysis, looking for signs that the cancer had spread. Breast cancer travels through the lymphatic system to find a new place to rest and multiply. When it has found a secondary site it metastasizes. This is bad news, otherwise known as 'secondaries' or 'secondary cancer'.

So 'spread' or even 'local spread' alarms them. They bring

in the big guns: the chemotherapy and a hormone treatment called Tamoxifen.

I was keen to know the score, but again had to wait for a diagnosis because the Consultant was on holiday and this time they weren't even hinting at the answer. Mr C is nothing but a playboy, I thought, bitterly. He's probably sailing in St Tropez right this minute.

I looked up the words 'diagnosis' and 'prognosis' so as to understand the difference.

Before this all started, I was waiting for a *diag*nosis, which, according to the dictionary, is 'the act or process of identifying or determining the nature and cause of a disease or injury through evaluation of patient history, examination and review of laboratory data.' This time, I was waiting for a *prog*nosis, which is 'the patient's chance of recovery.' It's much shorter. And much more scary.

At the beginning of this adventure it was very obvious to me what the diagnosis was going to be, but this time I had no clue.

Either the cancer had all been contained in the breast that was removed, in which case they would pronounce me cancer-free, or it had spread, in which case they would... what? Try to save my life.

In fact the waiting wasn't so hard this time. The days passed in a haze as I struggled with pain and infection.

I finally appeared in the Outpatients Clinic at my local hospital seventeen days after the operation.

Mr C was stern when I came into the room and jumped straight to the point. There was no preliminary softening of the blow. 'We removed thirteen lymph nodes from your armpit and the first three were infected with cancer,' he said.

He seemed to be glaring at me. He was probably distressed on my behalf, but I didn't understand that. I thought he was angry. Was it my fault? I almost said sorry.

He continued.

'We are going to recommend a course of chemotherapy treatment to you.'

I stopped breathing.

'What?'

'I'm telling you that the cancer has spread.'

'And what is my prognosis?'

His answer echoed around the room and bounced off the walls.

'The statistic that applies to you,' he said, 'is that if you take one hundred women in your age group with your degree of disease and roughly similar medical histories, and look at them in ten years time, fifty of them will be dead.'

So... he was saying I had a 50/50 chance of surviving ten years. Nice.

What's that saying about statistics? Oh yes. There are lies, damned lies and then there are statistics.

30 October 1996

Dear Dr I

I would be most grateful for your review of this pleasant woman. Dr H saw her at the Combined Clinic in August when a diagnosis of multifocal disease was made in her left breast.

She has now undergone a left mastectomy, axillary clearance and primary tram flap reconstruction.

Histology shows multifocal disease with a combination of both Grade 1 and Grade 2, the maximum diameter of the largest tumour being 22mm. She has involvement of three of thirteen lymph nodes retrieved from the axillary clearance specimen.

She is very well-read and I am not sure whether or not she will agree to chemotherapy but I would be grateful for your opinion and recommendations to her. I will keep her under regular review in any case.

With many thanks.

Yours sincerely,

Mr C

Consultant Surgeon

Cc Dr A

Cc Mr D

5 November 1996

Dear Mr C

Thank you for referring Janice to us whom I saw in clinic today. Janice underwent a left mastectomy and axillary clearance 2 weeks ago and the pathology showed multifocal disease with a combination of grade I and grade II disease, with a maximum diameter of the tumour being 22 mm. In addition she had 3/13 lymph nodes involved with tumour. She has recovered well from the surgery although has had a problem with a localized haematoma which had become infected.

I have had a long discussion with Janice and her husband

regarding the pros and cons of chemotherapy at this point in time. She clearly is at high risk from recurrence given the 3/13 positive lymph nodes. I have been through the nature of our trial, the TRAFIC trial, comparing FEC chemotherapy vs infusional ECF. I have been through the side effects and the expected benefits of the treatment and she is going to consider these over the next little while. I feel that it is likely however that she will enter onto the trial and receive chemotherapy. We will keep you informed of her decision.

Yours sincerely

Dr K

Senior Registrar to Dr E, Consultant Cancer Physician

'Doctor, Doctor, can I have a second opinion?' 'Of course you can. Come back tomorrow.'

1685, King Charles II

'The King was bled to the extent of a pint from a vein in his right arm. Next, his shoulder was cut into and the incised area was sucked of an additional 8oz of blood. An emetic and a purgative were administered followed by a second purgative followed by an enema containing antimony, sacred bitters, rock salt, mallow leaves, violets, beetroot, camomile flowers, fennel seeds, linseed, cinnamon, cardamom seed, saffron, cochineal and aloes.

The King's scalp was shaved and a blister raised. A sneezing powder of hellebore was administered. A plaster of burgundy pitch and pigeon dung was applied to the feet. Medicaments included melon seeds, manna, slippery elm, black cherry water, lime flowers, lily of the valley, peony, lavender and dissolved pearls. As he grew worse, forty drops of extract of human skull were administered, followed by a rallying dose of Raleigh's antidote. Finally Bezoar Stone was given.

Curiously, his Majesty's strength seemed to wane after all these interventions and, as the end of his life seemed imminent, his doctors tried a last-ditch attempt by forcing more Raleigh's mixture, pearl julep and ammonia down the dying King's throat. Further treatment was rendered more difficult by the King's death.'

Buckman, Robert, Magic or Medicine, Pan Books, 1994
Quoted in 'Great News on Cancer in the 21st Century' by Steven Random

I needed to decide about the chemotherapy. They told me that if it was to be really effective, the treatment should be started within six weeks of the operation.

I listened. I exhibited signs of intelligence and extreme courage in the face of adversity; I'd been practising. I asked questions. I signed a form saying that I would take part in a trial, which meant that I would be given the much sought-after prize of a 'Hickman line', a device which was designed to drip the chemotherapy straight into my bloodstream constantly and less intrusively than huge doses every three weeks.

I read the literature I had been given by the Mavericks. There were articles copied from a magazine called 'What the Doctors Don't Tell You', which said that there is evidence to suggest that chemotherapy causes secondary cancer in some cases. One article claimed that treatments for breast cancer had not advanced in effectiveness since the 1970s. Another said that chemotherapy was based on mustard gas. I rang a couple of the ladies from the group and tried to find out exactly what their diagnosis had been and why they had not accepted the chemotherapy treatment. I was looking for a reason why they had refused and why I should not.

They couldn't offer me that. Their cancers had been worse than mine, their spread had been worse and yet they had turned down the treatment.

'Why?' I asked.

'Because I didn't think it would work,' said one. 'I didn't think it was the best thing I could do for my body,' said the other.

I marvelled at this. If it hadn't been for that support group with their crazy life-enhancing ideas, it wouldn't have occurred to me that I could refuse the treatment. If it hadn't been for their articles and videos, I would never have gathered that anti-chemo information.

My whole being screamed at me not to have it. I had never been happy about putting drugs into my body, even the jolly kind, with which I experimented briefly at university, and definitely not the abusive kind. I didn't even take the Pill.

So how could I agree to chemotherapy?

I thought it would be like calling in the SAS because I'd found a rat living in the back of my sofa. A rat would be terrifying, yes, but... the SAS? They'd certainly kill the rat, but, in the fight, what would become of my living room?

Cancer is a disease of the immune system. So why would anyone treat it by attacking the immune system?

My treatment had scary names: 5FU, epirubicin, a cysplatin

trial, cyclophosphamide. I asked about the side effects. They told me. Nausea, vomiting, ulcers, diarrhoea, hair loss, low blood count causing dizziness, infection, inability to clot…

I am not an academic or any kind of a scholar. I am intuitive, right-brain-heavy and the child of my mother, who thinks that walking about with nothing on your feet when you are menstruating will give you a cold in the kidneys.

QED, my opinions may be questionable, coming as I do from a long line of madwomen, but it occurred to me that if the articles I had read were true – if, in the case of breast cancer, chemotherapy had not advanced in effectiveness since the 1970s, and if there really was evidence to show that in some cases it was actually harmful – what possible reason could I have for agreeing to it?

I didn't know what to do. But it was an important decision, perhaps the most important decision of my life, with a ticking clock attached.

The doctors had told me that if I didn't have the chemotherapy in that crucial six weeks after the operation it might be less effective, maybe not effective at all.

It wasn't an easy choice. I didn't want to do it, but if I didn't take the advice of the men in the white coats, then maybe the cancer would come back and bump me off. On the surface I appeared completely sure in my rejection of the treatment, and in many ways I was, but at the back of my mind there was a little voice asking: 'Are you, or are you not, being a completely irresponsible, brainless idiot?'

Oh, how I yearned for the days of yore; the days of yesteryear, the olden days, the golden days; the long hot summer days of my childhood, when I had no life-threatening illnesses, when I couldn't even conceive of such a thing because I was going to live forever – we were all going to live forever, me and Suze and Fat Bea and Patsy Parkin – and though the inside of my house was a war zone, the world outside it was nirvana.

'Those were the days my friend,' sang Mary Hopkin prophetically, the days when I had no disintegrating marriages and bad parenting on my conscience, no failed careers and expectations; no hazy, drunken, embarrassing adolescence to regret; when all I had to do was pitch up with my pals, lie beside a babbling brook and chew on a piece of long grass…

Oh for those days, when the hardest decision I had to make was whether or not to join Patsy Parkin's Rudey Club.

1964 Patsy Parkin and the Rudey Club

To get to Patsy's I had to leave my estate, walk around the grassy roundabout, past Mrs Bird's on the corner, down Courtlands Road where Andy Jones lived with The Straw, and into the cycle path at the bottom. At the end of the cycle path I would turn left and walk along past the row of little cottages and the corner shop, although, come to think of it, the corner shop wasn't actually on a corner. Then it was past the Methodist Sunday School where I used to go on my own when I was little, and left into Patsy's cycle path.

Halfway up Patsy's cycle path was another, on the right, which provided a short passageway into the bottom of her road. After that, a long, hot, tedious walk up the road to her house.

If I was feeling brave or in a hurry, I cut across the vast, flat allotment that joined my cycle path to hers and then followed her cycle path up the back of the houses in her street – although it seemed to go on for ever and it was a bit scary to try and remember which gate led into the back of her house.

On this particular day I braved the short cut and met Patsy in the allotment. She was obviously in a funny mood. In accordance with tradition, she had a small boy with her.

Small boys came and went in our lives; they were two a penny. In those days there were always smaller children around. They were allowed out on their own because it was accepted that they would hang out with the older children, learning the ropes of survival: how to cross roads; how to build a den; how to play ancient games passed down like skipping and tag; how to find all the 'secret places' in the area and generally how to survive the badlands outside their own homes. Every generation of children brought up the next and taught them to play safely outside the house.

I asked Patsy what they were up to and she said that if they told me, I would have to keep it a deadly secret. I promised.

'It's a rudey club,' she said. The small boy nodded.

'What have you got to do?' I asked, getting straight to the point.

'You've got to wee on the ground. You've got to sit in the fork of this tree and do a wee on the ground and then you can join.'

'What do you get for joining?' I said.

'Stuff,' promised Patsy.

I shook my head.

'Why not?' she asked.

I shook my head again.

'Go on,' she said. 'It's easy.'

'You do it then.'

'I have.'

'Do it again, then.' I was adamant. I wasn't going to be made a monkey of, made to sit half naked in the fork of a tree and wee on the ground, while they ran off laughing.

Patsy sighed heavily, rolled her eyes at the small boy – who rolled his eyes right back at her – and pulled off her jeans. She heaved herself up into the tree and sat at the apex of two branches with her legs wide apart and hooked over each. I went and stood behind her. I had no desire to gaze at Patsy's winkle, as the small boy seemed to want to do.

Shocked to my core, I watched the yellow stream of wee falling to form a gilded puddle beneath her. I felt quite sick. I didn't want to join their horrible rudey club. I thought the whole thing was very rude indeed. But I hadn't known Patsy long and I didn't want her to think I wasn't fun.

I couldn't speak. I didn't want to do it, really didn't want to, but I pulled down my pants and hauled myself up into the tree, gingerly avoiding the wet earth beneath. It was a very uncomfortable position to hold for any length of time, but my wretched bladder just wouldn't perform.

I waited and strained and tried and sent stern commands to my groin, but it was no good, nothing would come.

'Hurry up,' said Patsy.

'I'm trying,' I said, humiliation creeping over me to join the distaste I already felt. I got cross, and then I got down.

'Come on,' said Patsy, 'don't give up.'

'I don't want to.'

'Well, you can't join our club then.'

'Don't want to,' I said, back on terra firma *and feeling sure of myself again. 'I don't want to join your stupid rudey club.'*

'All right. Don't then. Come on,' she said to her little henchman, who stuck his tongue out at me by way of goodbye and they marched off.

Happy days: long gone.

And here I was again, being asked to join a rudey club, of sorts, which would make my hair fall out and ulcers grow in my mouth and on my hands, and make me throw up. Not unlike Patsy's club. And membership of the Chemo Club seemed to offer the same promise of what I would get if I joined, which was a big fat nothing; only the possibility of 'stuff'.

In this case, the possibility of survival.

The Case Against

Of course the doctors wouldn't give up without a fight. So I returned fire.

I said, 'How can I put the children through that? Six months of me being like a zombie, when they've already had to put up with me being turned into a Frankenstein lookalike.'

'Chemotherapy is based on mustard gas,' I said.

'Chemotherapy sometimes causes secondary cancer,' I said.

'Having chemotherapy is like getting the SAS to clear a rat from your living room.' They usually looked a little bemused when I said that one.

'Chemotherapy has consistently failed to make a really

significant impact on breast cancer since the 1970s,' I said, which was true in 1996.

'If I had testicular cancer, for which disease the success rate of chemotherapy is 97%, then I would very probably agree to it, but I don't.'

'And what's more, you don't have testicles,' said the intellectually challenged amongst them.

'That's not the point,' I said. 'Chemotherapy is abusive, it's wrong, it's horrible and I am not going to do that to my body.'

But even while I was arguing, my own inner voice continued to gnaw at me. Was I doing the right thing?

I requested an interview at the cancer centre with the chemotherapy specialist, Dr I. I wanted to be as sure as I could be; I wanted to hear the opinion of the great man himself.

I took Mark and a sensible friend called Mary, who admitted later that she came willingly because she wanted to try and influence me to have the chemo.

The interview started with Dr I steaming through the side-effects of chemotherapy, expecting that they were at the heart of my discontent.

I interrupted him. 'I know the symptoms. That's not why I'm here. I'm here for you to give me a reason to have the treatment.' And I told him what I had learned from the Mavericks and from my own research. The atmosphere in the room changed suddenly. He sat up – literally – and took notice. So I wasn't just a silly woman, afraid of the side effects. Little did he know I was that too; but not just that.

He listened to my arguments and I listened to his. He

didn't have many. So then I asked him the sixty-four thousand dollar question.

'What difference will it make to my prognosis?'

'It will change your fifty/fifty chance of survival by five percent,' said the Consultant.

Five percent? Only five percent?

Sod that for a game of soldiers.

I said 'No.'

'No?!' said the Registrar.

'No?!' said the Consultant.

'No?!' said all my friends, my husband and my family. 'Did you say, "No"?'

'Yes,' I said. 'Thanks very much, but no.'

On the day of that visit to the hospital, the Consultant said that he was impressed at how thoroughly I had investigated the subject.

'Research has been carried out into the placebo effect,' he said, 'and it has been found to be a strong factor in healing.' I nodded. I knew a little about this myself. I knew that he was thinking that whatever treatment I had, I needed to believe in it, hook, line and sinker.

'If I were you,' he went on, 'thinking and feeling as you do, I would very probably turn down the chemotherapy myself.'

So I turned it down.

26 November 1996

Dear Mr C

I caught up with this lady today who was seen in my absence at her last visit by my colleague Dr K. You will remember that she had a breast cancer but with 3/13 lymph nodes involved.

She has had a long time to think about chemotherapy and her decision is that she would rather not have this treatment. I am very happy that she understands all the implications here. We had a long talk covering the fact that adjuvant chemotherapy statistically has been shown to increase survival by a modest amount.

Her own feeling is that she can do just as well and perhaps better with lifestyle changes aimed at boosting her immune system. By the same token she does not wish adjuvant Tamoxifen. She would like to 'leave the door open' to the Centre and I have assured her that we work closely together and I would be happy to see her at any time in the future should problems arise.

Yours sincerely

Dr I, Consultant Cancer Physician

Going it Alone

For a few months after making the decision to refuse the chemical treatment I was irritatingly evangelical about my life-changes, dined out on the story of how I'd turned down the chemo loudly and often, until one day I found myself listening to someone else for once.

By a bizarre coincidence she had the same cancer as me, the same degree of aggression, she was the same age, had the same Consultant, the same operation, the same prognosis and the same offer of treatment.

And she too had asked the sixty-four thousand dollar question, 'What difference will the chemotherapy make to my chances of survival?'

Not surprisingly, he gave her the same answer he'd given me: five percent.

I waited eagerly to hear the end of this story, already nodding in anticipation that her answer would be the same as mine. I asked her what she had replied to the Consultant and she told me.

'Five percent! That's brilliant! I'll do it.'

I straightened up. I gaped at her, for once momentarily lost for words. I struggled to respond.

'Well… there's a funny thing. Five percent eh? Isn't that fantastic?'

She certainly thought it was. After we had parted I mulled it over. It was certainly an interesting way to look at it; not my way exactly, but everybody's different. And like the Consultant said, whatever treatment we choose, we'll give ourselves the best chance of survival if we believe it will work.

It's horses for courses, that's all. Horses for courses.

And so there I was, trudging the road to happy destiny with my 50/50 chance of surviving the next ten years all wrapped up in a red spotted kerchief and tied to a stick.

I had turned my back on the warm embrace of the medical profession, waved goodbye to the big fat momma that is the NHS and decided to go it alone.

Oops.

'Well here's another nice mess you've gotten me into...'

Laurel and Hardy 'Sons of the Desert' 1933

My original notebook entitled 'Getting Abreast of Things' was worn and tattered. I decided that the situation was serious enough to merit a whole file. It was only a bog-standard lever arch file but I stuck a couple of pictures of cherubs on it from old Christmas cards to gain some Brownie points with God. (I was still hedging my bets with the God concept, just in case God had anything to do with this.)

I created three sections, one each for Mind, Body and Spirit. Then I began my campaign.

The grand plan was to continue to read literature about cancer and nutrition; to go back into therapy to struggle with and eventually embrace my demons; and to boldly set out on that long journey of a thousand miles that begins with one small step: my spiritual path.

That was the plan, anyway.

But first things first. I sat down and wrote a story, an allegory of my experiences, by way of marshalling my thoughts.

The Princess and the Wise Woman

Once upon a time, a beautiful princess was struck down by an ugly disease. She took it to the white-coats. They said a bad thing was growing inside her and gave her medicine that made her feel ill.

Then the one with the big knife came and cut her into little pieces. She thanked him, for she was polite as well as beautiful.

He sewed her back together with hemp and it hurt for a long time.

'Why has this happened to me?' she wailed. They shrugged.

'I did do bad things,' she said. 'I worked too hard. I played too hard. I ate sugar and fat by day and drank whisky by night. I smoked the weed and didn't sleep and it's all my fault.'

'No! No! No!' they said. 'It isn't all your fault.'

'You mean some of it is,' she said.

'No!' said the one with the knife. 'It's simply that cancer occurs where genetic vulnerability meets environmental abuse, d'you see? So one's culpability is certainly worthy of debate but on no account to be admitted.'

'Pardon?'

'Just don't do it again.'

'Oh, right. I shan't. Don't worry.'

She went to consult a wise woman, found in Yellow Pages, and told her the whole story.

'This experience is a gift,' began the wise woman.

'Thank you very much,' said the princess, 'but I don't want it.'

'It is the gift of Life. Take it and be grateful.'

'I thought I was already alive,' said the princess.

'You weren't,' said the wise woman, 'trust me.'

No bloody fear, thought the princess. I trusted God and God gave me an ugly disease. I trusted the man with the knife and he poisoned me, cut me, refashioned me, sewed me, stapled me, and finally photographed me for his files. Why should I trust a woman who calls this a gift? The princess thought about leaving.

On the other hand, she mused, if she is confident enough

to advertise in the Yellow Pages, then she is certainly more confident than I am.

The princess decided to stay. She smiled encouragingly at the wise woman, who held up a book called Beating Cancer with Nutrition by Dr Patrick Quillin and quoted: 'Cancer is like a light flashing in the dashboard of a faulty car. It says "Pull this car over and fix it now."'

I do hate those cars that talk to you, thought the princess.

'You have been given the opportunity to change,' said the woman. 'Do so, and your life will be enriched beyond your wildest dreams. Fail to do so and you will very probably die.'

The princess was shocked. 'I don't wish to appear rude,' she said, folding her arms and sniffing, 'but who are you to tell me this?'

'I am someone who has been through it herself.' The wise woman smiled, wisely.

Huh, thought the princess, we'll see about that. 'You mean you've had a mastectomy?' she challenged.

'Yes.'

'Well… I've had a mastectomy and reconstruction as well.'

'Yes, I had a reconstruction. In fact, I had a double mastectomy and reconstruction.'

'Oh.' The princess was temporarily stumped. Then she reloaded. 'Which did you opt for? A trans-abdominal? Or a latissimus dorsi? I mean to say,' she paused and attempted to smile wisely herself before continuing, 'were the new breasts made out of your stomach flap, or the big muscles at the top of your back?'

'They were made out of fat from my stomach flap,' the wise

woman replied, 'and the big rectus abdominis muscles. They were folded over diagonally and pulled up to my new breasts so that they had a ready-made blood supply, a bit like a cross-your-heart bra. Remember those?'

The princess began to shrink. 'My lymph nodes were infected,' she said, desperately. 'Thirteen were removed. Three were cancerous.'

'Twenty-four removed; seventeen infected,' retorted the wise woman.

'What about the cancer?' snapped the princess. 'Mine was grade two; moderate growth; invasive ductal.'

The wise woman shook her head and sighed. 'Nothing so simple, I'm afraid. Mine was grade three; aggressive; and invasive lobular.'

The princess gasped. Aggressive? Crikey!

'Prognosis?' She hardly dared ask.

'Less than a year,' said the wise woman, 'But that was ten years ago and here I am still. Hale and hearty!' She laughed and it was all over. The wise woman had won her right to be heard.

The princess picked up her shiny pink notebook, labelled 'Getting Abreast of Things'. At the top of a new page she wrote 'Local Wisdom' in large letters.

'I'm listening,' she said, pen poised. 'What shall I do?'

'You must change. Most importantly, change your habits.'

'How?'

'Fresh air, exercise, fruit, fibre and vegetables. Change your household products for safe ones. Cut out sugar, caffeine, and alcohol. No stimulants of any kind must pass your lips. Of course you don't smoke?'

The princess shook her head and wrote 'Help me', thinking that she might wrap the page around a rock and throw it out of the window. The wise woman poured her a glass of water. 'Drink plenty of this,' she said, handing over the glass. 'If you can drink a couple of glasses of water first thing in the morning, and then jump up and down on a mini-trampoline, you will find that you want to go.'

'Go where?'

'You will find out.'

She gently nudged a piece of paper across the table. 'Get these,' she said. It was a list of books. The princess picked it up and looked at the first three names on the list. 'Chicken Soup for the Soul'; 'Feel the Fear and Do It Anyway'; 'You Can Heal Your Life'.

'What's all this?' she said.

The wise woman went on. 'You must visit healers, natural healers and spiritual healers; also herbalists, aromatherapists, psychotherapists and hypnotherapists. Then there are naturopaths and, naturally, homeopaths.'

'Psychopaths...' wrote the princess and looked around the room for a clock. There were none.

'To sum up,' continued the wise woman, 'You must learn about nutrition and care for your body. Take vitamins and supplements. Eat tons of vegetables. More vegetables than you can possibly imagine. Eat them. And you must begin to love yourself and let go of all your resentment. Cancer thrives on resentment.'

'What do you mean?' asked the princess. 'I have no resentment.' She bit her thumbnail and looked shifty.

The wise woman smiled. 'The books will explain. You'll see.' She leaned forward in her chair. The princess also leaned forward, wondering if she was finally going to hear the secret of the wise woman's survival.

'If you had mould growing in your bathroom,' the woman whispered, 'you'd attack it with chemicals. And then you'd scrub it all away, wouldn't you?'

'Er... yes,' said the princess, wondering why the woman was whispering.

'But if you didn't get rid of the warm, damp conditions in the room, the mould would come back.' She leant back in her chair. 'See?'

'Er... no.'

The wise woman leaned forward again, and spoke slowly. 'You must destroy the environment in which the cancer thrives.'

'Destroy the environment... but that's me!'

'Yes. You've got it.' She relaxed into her chair and smiled. 'It's already begun. Just keep up the good work.'

The princess stared at her, until the wise woman stood up and gestured towards the door. 'Get the books,' she said. 'Then you'll understand. Learn to love yourself. Forgive yourself. Let go of the resentment. Cancer thrives on resentment.'

The princess was angry. On the doorstep, she turned back and spoke with a slight edge to her voice; and very nearly, despite the years of training and control, revealed the strength of her feelings. 'You said I should destroy myself in order to survive. That's rubbish. That's just finishing the work of the man with the knife and all his white-coated pals.'

The wise woman smiled broadly. 'But the old you is already

dead. It was cut out of you. The new you, on the other hand, waits to blossom. Let it, and turn your life into a masterpiece. You might not survive, but at least you'll have tried.'

The princess knew that being angry was pointless. She finally asked what she really wanted to know.

'How did you survive?'

She was surprised when the wise woman shrugged, just as the white-coats had shrugged when she asked them why she had got cancer. 'How do I know?' she said. 'Everyone dies eventually.' She leaned against the doorframe. 'It just seems to me that some people die on the first day. Some people lie down and wait for the hearse. I didn't. I wanted to live. And here I am.'

The princess couldn't speak. She felt something odd happening. Something strange but familiar touched her; she wasn't sure what it was but it was from the distant past, something that children feel... Oh yes of course, she did know. It was hope; the feeling that all things are possible. She remembered a poem by Emily Dickinson and spoke slowly, half to herself.

'Hope is the thing with feathers, that perches in the soul; and sings the tune without the words; and never stops, at all.'

The wise woman smiled at her and for the first time the princess smiled back. 'Do you know what?' she said. 'I'm going to have that painted above the picture rail in my bedroom!'

'That's the ticket,' said the wise woman. 'You've got it.' The wise woman straightened up and clapped her hands together. It was time to go.

'Same time next week, Princess?'

'Yes, please,' said the princess, and crossed the woman's palm with a twenty-pound note. She turned to go... but stopped.

Biting her lip for a moment, she made her confession.
  'To tell you the truth... I'm not really a princess.'
  'Oh, but you are,' said the wise woman. 'Definitely.'

The Right Frame of Mind

One day when I was brushing my teeth I caught sight of my woebegone reflection in the bathroom mirror. This won't do, I thought. It won't do at all.

I stood up straight and shot from the hip.

'Listen up. If you agree that the worse state of being is death; and the best state of being is a life which as near as dammit resembles a state of bliss, where you have no financial cares at all, a job which offers joyful Monday mornings, children who are totally rewarding and not all the other things that children are – nothing like your children anyway – no emotional problems, an idyllic love match with your partner and perfect health... Have I left anything out?

My reflection pretended to think about it. But I didn't wait. I was on a roll.

'So, anyway, if you agree with that assessment of human existence, then everything that happens to you in life must appear somewhere on a scale between those two states of being. Right?

'And if that is true, if you count backwards from the state of death along that scale, you might find yourself thinking about things like being maimed, or horribly scarred, or having chronic pain, or suffering from a wasting disease or the one that eats your flesh...' I stopped for a moment, hardly able to think about that without cold fear freezing my limbs. But that was good: there existed a state of being for which I would not swap my current position.

'So if you think about it, you will find that there are many, many more horrible things that could happen to you, things that are worse than the state of being in which you find yourself at this particular moment.

'Have you got it?'

My reflection stared back. And nodded, slowly. I'd got it. But that didn't stop me driving the point home.

'What I'm trying to say is this: count your blessings while you may. Tomorrow your legs might drop off.'

It was all very inspiring. I even inspired myself. I decided that I was ready to go back to work and agreed to do a concert with *The Cotton Club Orchestra*, though I wasn't ready: neither physically nor emotionally. I managed to get through it but inside I was in bits. Of course I was grateful to have survived the operation but still couldn't look at my scars properly in a mirror. It was a dark period for me.

People kept telling me how much they admired the fact that I didn't wear my cancer like a badge.

I did wear it though. I wore it under my clothes.

The Bird of Paradise

'This is your thirty-minute call, Miss Day.'

Thirty minutes. Just time for a shower, a really hot one if the shower worked. I tried it. Yes, great, it did. Hot, really hot. I turned round and round, letting the water soothe me into oblivion, as it did when I came out of hospital.

Out of the shower, I could hear some of the band laughing

in the next room. It was great being the girl singer because I was sometimes given a dressing room to myself while all ten men squashed into a room the same size.

It was a rare luxury though, to have a room. More often than not, my dressing room was the loo.

I wasn't expecting a shower so I only had the little hand-towel I kept in my gig-bag. My eyes caught my reflection as I undressed. Ouch, there was my belly in the mirror. What a mess.

A thick red scar ran right across it where they took the fat.

I remembered the plastic surgeon. 'There's a lot of you, isn't there?' he'd said as he considered how he was going to reinvent me.

Then I was dry and my little towel was soaking wet. I refused to look in the mirror. I busied myself, putting out my makeup. I always did this to calm myself down before going on. I arranged it all in order: first the foundation, then the powder, then the blusher, the eye-makeup, the eye pencil, the eyebrow pencil, and finally, my favourite, the lipstick. It was all arranged and standing on end, my private army, waiting to do my bidding.

Our eyes met in the mirror, that body's and mine. I could see the breast at the edge of my vision. *Don't look at the breast!* Oh God, there it was. A breast without a nipple. What was that? What was the good of that?

Concentrate, I told myself. *Put on your watch. That's the first thing to be done.*

I felt an urge to cover myself up but resisted angrily. *I'm not ashamed*, I thought. *I am not going to make a point of putting*

*on my clothes when I have always enjoyed walking about naked.
I just won't look, that's all.*

Twenty minutes to go. Right, I needed to get on with it. I
unpacked my clothes and began to drape them over the tatty
old chair: always a slightly difficult exercise for me because I
had to think backwards. Last on, first down. First the gig coat.
Then the green Lurex dress.

The 'gig coat' was made especially for me by a designer. It
cost the enormous sum of £600. It was my *pièce de resistance*
and covered up the less flattering green lurex dress; also
made especially for me, though this time by a seamstress in
Shepherd's Bush, for fifty quid.

The two together created a masterpiece. The glowing
emerald green peeped out shyly between the two edges of the
severe, black crepe gig-coat with the heavily beaded shoulders
and transformed into... The Fat Lady in the Lovely Green
Dress.

After the green dress came the corset. I was ashamed of
still having to wear a corset. I didn't get the flat tummy I had
imagined would come with the fashioning of my breast from
my stomach. I got a hernia instead.

The tights, the bra and the knickers went last on the chair,
being first on the body.

Fifteen minutes to go and I was all set, more or less, though
still not dressed or made-up. Someone knocked at the door.

'Janice?'

'Yes?'

'Are you all right?'

'Yes.'

165

'OK.'

It was just the bass player. He went off. My eyes met their reflection in the mirror: wide, afraid. Guard down suddenly, mouth set, I decided to look.

There it was. The breast. There was the red scar going around the top of the breast and the line running under the armpit. For an insane moment I thought it looked like a nipple, a huge white one. But not really. It wasn't a nipple. There was no nipple. I looked exactly the same as I always had, but there was no nipple, just the thick red line making a three-inch-wide circle around the top of the breast.

Like the nightmare, I thought, remembering a childhood dream. It was a woman with no face; just a blank space where the mouth, nose and eyes should be. That's what my breast looked like.

Further down was the homemade tummy button, creased as if it had been badly ironed. What is that tummy button supposed to be, I thought.

But I couldn't complain, *I mustn't complain.* I was still alive, wasn't I?

People said I was brave. Why? What would anyone say if they were told they had breast cancer; that they needed to have a mastectomy right away?

They would say, 'Oh.' What else could they say?

'Oh.'

Well, according to my friends, that was really brave.

And if someone told them they have a fifty-percent chance of surviving the next ten years, they would say, 'Right. Thank you.' Wouldn't they?

Was that brave? Was it really brave not to sob and scream the whole day long? Was it brave to go about my business, behaving normally, when I really wanted to scream at the top of my voice that nothing anybody else said or did was of any interest to me whatsoever, that the only thing that mattered was my illness, my chances of living or dying; my pain, my fear, me!!

Not revealing any of that was called brave. I called it a big fat lie.

'This is your ten minute call, Miss Day.'

Oh shit. Paralysis. Guard down again, my eyes met with their reflection in the mirror.

Why did you do this to me?

What else could I do?

You could have prayed and chanted affirmations, you could have detoxified. You could have had healing every day and colon cleansing and done Tai Chi. You didn't have to turn me into a monster from a B-movie. It hurt too; like a thousand papercuts. You didn't have to do it.

Oh stop it. They had to cut it out, didn't they? At least you've got two breasts; you don't have an implant and you have a damn sight less tummy than you had before. What's more, you haven't got a congenitally fat arse. Could you muster up a little bit of gratitude for that, maybe?

The eyes, angry and sullen, slid away. Come on, I said to myself, shake this off. Get ready, quickly. I hurried into my clothes. Knickers, bra, corset, tights, dress, coat. Done it. Where are my shoes, where are my bloody shoes? Good, the adrenalin has come at last. Can't perform without adrenalin...

Makeup. Calm, calm, calm. I needed a steady hand.

Someone shouted through the door.

'See you down there!'

'I'm just coming!'

They trooped past my door, still telling jokes. Why can't men have conversations? Maybe it's just musicians, I don't know.

Foundation came next. Slapped on, blended and then powdered.

Ah, there she was. Emerging in the mirror, with her great black eyes and red cheeks, her eyebrows arched and wobbly. And then, last of all, those beautiful, bright red curvy lips... I had reinvented myself. I was ready.

I walked down to the stage before my final call with just the right amount of fear and just the right amount of calm. Then I paced, as I always did; up and down, wringing my hands endlessly; driving the stage manager mad with my pacing up and down, up and down.

I prayed, as I always do, to keep my ego at bay, whispering to myself, '*This is for the glory of God and the pleasure of the assembled company*,' and then I paced again; letting the music thrill me, the beat of the drums permeating my consciousness and taking me over; letting my throat open up and filling my lungs with air... until...

Ah, there it was – the intro – then the applause and off I went! It was all there, all ready, and the brave, lovely and glamorous songbird took her place on the stage of life – Ha! Ha! – to entertain and titillate the grateful public.

You know what they say about glamour? The closer you

come to glamour, the harder it is to find. But to the audience, in that moment, I was all glamour; I was glamour personified, like a beautiful bright Bird of Paradise, and I belonged to them.

And as I walked across to the microphone and heard the applause crashing in glorious waves around the auditorium, waves of love that for a time would fill the aching hole inside me, a single thought flashed across my mind, clear as a bell; a daft rhyming couplet that dropped into my head all-of-a-piece and said it all...

"Cause nobody knows, and never will guess, what lies underneath the lovely green dress.'

Bonkers... but Understandable

Mark had opposed the more complex reconstruction, the belly-to-breast operation. He had wanted me to have the simplest op and think about dealing with the tummy later. I thought he was being a poo-faced meanie as usual and wouldn't listen to him. I was only concerned with getting rid of my big fat belly.

Strangely, Mark wasn't impressed with this plan, pointing out that it was a major operation which would probably hurt terribly. I smiled a beatific smile, thinking of those pencil-slim skirts at the back of the wardrobe.

'Why don't you have the easier one,' he'd pleaded, 'where they just pull the back muscle round to the front and turn it into the new breast? Then we can save up for a tummy tuck when you've recovered.'

'What planet are you on?' I said. 'Do you think I'm going

to go through all this and get nothing out of it except a sore back?'

Yes it was bonkers, but it was understandable.

Breast cancer in women comes with a double whammy. Not only do we have to deal with the fact that we might die, but we also have to deal with the attack on our body image, our femininity and our sense of who we are.

All women are different. Some are born beautiful, some grow to beauty and some – with enough money – have beauty thrust upon them… Of course, there's such a thing as inner beauty, though I could see no sign of that in my mirror. Blessed indeed are the women who don't give a damn how they look. Not me, alas. At least, not then.

Before I contracted cancer I was a Mum, the sort that's covered in sick and permanently welded inside a pair of black leggings. I was also unhappily overweight and hated my belly, so I wasn't exactly starting from a level playing field.

It wasn't that the operation threatened my sexual identity. I was never in any doubt that I was a woman, with or without breasts or any number of nipples. But could I think of myself as an attractive woman again? Aye, there was the rub. Especially as I had already given up on that possibility even before the cancer, at the tender age of 39.

So even though I was going to lose my natural breast and expected to be horribly scarred, I was almost thrilled about the tummy tuck because it seemed to offer me a path back to the physical beauty I believed was lost to me for ever.

Of course it was daft. I knew I couldn't turn back Time. I just thought I might give it go.

And why? Being pretty, nubile and fatherless had its disadvantages.

1969 The Man who Followed me Home

At twelve, I lurked behind thick wings of hair and a bushy fringe. I wanted to hide myself. I felt ugly, and nothing seemed to fit, least of all the various parts of my body. I hated my carroty hair; I hated my vast hips and the two round bumps on my chest. I hated the fact that my clothes didn't hang properly, that my armpits wilfully and viciously perspired, and that I blushed scarlet whenever a man spoke to me. I hated all the changes that continued to assault my once proud child-body.

Only my love of roller-skating lured me into the open. On Saturday mornings, Patsy, Kathy Carter and I braved the stares of strangers and went to skate at the Corn Exchange, the large communal building in Newbury marketplace. I couldn't do fancy manoeuvres, couldn't waltz or go backwards very well, but I was fast. I could cross one leg over the other as I went around the corner and flew like a bird, weaving in and out of other mere mortals with stunning grace.

One day, a tall, thin, scruffy-haired man approached me and bought me a pop. He was persistent, whispering compliments, saying that I should always tie my hair up; that it was a shame to cover up the pretty face that emerged when my hair flew back. He whispered that I skated better than anyone else there; looked better than anyone else there; that I was, in truth, better than anyone else there.

He followed Kathy Carter and me home across the park, all the while whispering and flattering; making my head spin. I couldn't stop the smile pulling at the corners of my mouth. I barely looked at him, but I didn't want him to stop. I didn't want the fluttering feelings all over my body to stop.

'Are you a virgin?' he asked. I knew what that was. It was someone who had never done 'It'. What 'It' was, though, I hadn't the faintest idea, having missed the sex education course at school, and never having read my mother's little booklet.

When he asked if he could come into the house, since there was no one home, I saw no reason why not. And when he suggested that he and I should go somewhere private to talk, leaving poor Kathy Carter scarlet with embarrassment and alone on the sofa, I saw no reason why we shouldn't.

'Where are you going?' she said.

'He just wants to talk to me in private,' I said, and shrugged.

'What about?'

'I dunno,' I said, and followed him upstairs. I had no idea what was going to happen; I only knew that it felt nice. When he suggested that I would be more comfortable if I took off all my clothes and lay down on the bed, I thought that he was probably right, so I did.

But then he started to stroke me. I couldn't think why he was doing that. His hand went down to my private part, where the coarse ginger hair was growing, and I pushed it away. He lay on top of me. I felt squashed and told him so, and suddenly I felt uncomfortable about the whole thing and frightened.

'You know, I won't do anything that you don't want me to,' he whispered, and stroked, and the stroking felt ok then, because he wasn't going to do anything that I didn't want him to, and I said, 'Well, I don't want you to touch me down there,' and he said, 'Of course I won't, if you really don't want me to, although I think you'd like it,' and I thought about it, while he stroked me some more, and after a while I said, 'OK then, I don't mind,' and he said, 'Are you sure?' and I said, 'Well, I don't know, but you can try it if you like,' and then someone knocked on the door.

We sat bolt upright. I realised that I had been deluding myself that this was all completely innocent. Suddenly I didn't want anyone to know.

I felt caught out.

We sat, frozen with fright, as the door slowly opened. But it was all right. It was only Kathy Carter, still scarlet.

'Your sister is home,' she said.

'Where is she?'

'Downstairs, in the kitchen.'

We jumped up, threw on our clothes, and made a plan. Kathy and I would creep down first. I would go into the kitchen and distract Jane, and Kathy would let the man out.

As I turned away, the man held me and kissed me.

'Thank you,' he said. I looked at him, bemused, and wondered why he was thanking me. He hadn't got what he had come for, had he? He'd wanted to touch my private part and I hadn't let him. He'd wanted to lie on top of me and I had pushed him off.

But he thanked me.
He was, at least, polite.

Taking Stock

So there I was.

I had vanquished the Grim Reaper on the operating table;

I had recovered completely from the urine infection;

I had survived the infected haematoma;

I had won an Oscar for my performance in the 'I'm not having any chemotherapy' melodrama.

I had hidden out and healed up at home in the bosom of my family, pun intended.

Compared to bringing up children, it was a doddle. But now I was left with two problems. Two little ones.

I didn't want to die.

I didn't want to look like Frankenstein's cousin Julie.

In fact, I wanted to look as good as I could and having the free tummy tuck had seemed crucial to my plan. That's why I had the belly-to-breast op in the first place. But things hadn't gone quite as I'd hoped.

The breast orb itself was a smashing job: it was round and perfect, and healed with no puckering of the scars where the surgeon attached the skin from my belly onto what was left of my original breast.

But there were some hitches. The surgeon had warned me about them and he was right.

Firstly, they didn't put in the mesh which would have contained my abdomen once they had removed the muscle that had been designed to do that. The surgeon told me later that the mesh was a matter of choice. But I have my own theory. The operation took nine hours, and it is my belief that they went for a curry in the middle of it and when they got back found that they were clean out of meshes and it was just too late to nip out and buy some.

However it happened, doing without the mesh was not the right decision for me. Because I had 'poor muscle tone', which is a polite way of saying that I was flabby, the reconstruction left me with a surgical hernia in the lower abdomen that resulted in a bulge on my right side.

Secondly, whilst they cleverly created a tummy button for me – because the old one got lifted off with the rest of the flab – the new tummy button was slightly off-centre and strangely small.

And thirdly, they left a little flap of loose skin on the left of my abdomen, which they fondly called a 'dog-ear'.

So there I was, with only one nipple, an asymmetrical stomach, a tummy button that didn't look quite right, a dog's ear hanging from my belly and a pig's ear hanging from my chest.

I was a vision.

You're a Lardy-Arse, Missus, and No Mistake

4 January 1997

Dear Dr A

I reviewed Mrs Day today. The left breast reconstruction looks very good. There is some ptosis of the right breast which makes some clothing difficult, and this could be helped by a simple mastopexy. She does have a slight bulge in the right side of the abdomen, and probably has a hernia here, however the situation is not helped by her weight.

I have therefore asked her to lose three stone, and to come and see me in about four months' time, when I will review the situation.

Kind regards

Yours sincerely

Mr D, Consultant

Cc Mr C

'Doctor, Doctor, have you got something for a bad headache?' 'Of course. Just take this hammer and hit yourself in the head. Then you'll have a bad headache.'

I asked Mr D if he could please do something about the painful bulge in my stomach. It wasn't terribly painful, I said, just a bit, but it stuck out horribly. I was very self-conscious about it, I said.

Also, I continued, wanting to bolster my case, I was a danger to Society. He looked alarmed. I explained that whenever I sneezed I had to hold my stomach with both hands, otherwise it hurt. This meant that I was spraying everyone with my germs, which was a health hazard and making me unpopular. God forbid.

Mr D demurred. He wouldn't do it, he said, until I had lost at least a stone of my excess weight. I can't remember his reason, something about it being 'risky'. I was no longer listening. I lost consciousness when he mentioned 'morbid obesity'.

He pointed to his chart and said I was already obese and only a smidgeon away from morbid obesity. And this – as everybody knows – is not a good thing. The word 'morbid' has to do with death, doesn't it? Even if it doesn't actually mean death, it definitely hangs out with the word death on a regular basis. So 'morbidly obese', even to the ignorant, clearly means 'dangerously fat'.

I decided at once that I must do something… anything… about my weight. Anything, that is, apart from eating less.

'I will lose much more than a stone in a month,' I boasted wildly to the surgeon. He was disparaging about my ability to do that.

'Why do you think I won't?' I said.

'Well, some girls just don't make it,' he said.

I left in high dudgeon, insulted not only by his lack of faith in me but by him calling me a 'girl' at the sad old age of 39. Who was he kidding? I had left girlhood behind me and it was never coming back. And I didn't need to be reminded of that, thank you very much. Yes, I was definitely in high dudgeon and on my high horse and possibly high with rage.

I determined to prove him wrong. I think he was practising reverse psychology and was pleased with himself for stirring me up. 'That'll do the trick,' I expect he thought.

Well, it didn't. A month later, after rigorous, dedicated and devoted attempts at dieting, I was a stone heavier.

Even the knowledge that obesity and a high fat diet are linked with breast cancer hadn't galvanised me into losing weight. And once again, though I joked with my friends about my inability to stop over-eating, inside I was in pain – deep pain – as I saw the ever-widening gap between the beautiful, bright child I once was and the sorry creature I thought I had become.

Sugar Junkie

*'If I was alive in Rubens' time I wouldn't have to be a
comedienne for a living. I'd be celebrated as a beautiful
model. In those days Kate Moss would only have one use,
as a paintbrush. He'd be painting me and I'd say 'What's
that in your hand, Rubens?' He'd say 'It's Kate Moss. I'm
using her as a paintbrush.'*
Dawn French on Big Women (dawnfrenchonline.co.uk)

20 May 1997

Dear Dr A

I reviewed Mrs Day today. The left breast reconstruction
continues to look good. She has put on quite a lot of weight
and this is reflected in the increased size of the reconstructed
breast.

She still has a muscle hernia on the right side of the abdomen
and this could be repaired with a mesh. However, I would not
do it at the moment as her BMI is 31.

I suggested she comes to see me again when she has got her
weight down to about 11½ stone.

Kind regards

Yours sincerely

Mr D, Consultant

1957-1998 Mmmm... Donuts...

I was a sugar junky from a very early age. My Mum put
sugar in my milk, sugar on my sandwiches and honey on my

dummy. Mmm, absolutely yummy, Mummy. But strangely, that was the extent of her largesse. And she was large, was my old Mum. She was definitely a 'largesse' herself, just not in the area of treats. There were no cakes, biscuits or sweets anywhere in the house. Only sugar.

So it was almost a spiritual experience to visit Fat Bea and eat her mum's home-made lemon drizzle cake, lemon Madeira cake and double chocolate gateaux. We never had anything like that at home. It wasn't considered healthy. Mum's repertoire consisted of scrag-end stew and watery minced beef curry. Only the sugar sandwiches and the Sunday roast followed by apple pie and custard lit up our long dark days inside the house.

And Fat Bea, who – despite all the obvious advantages of a cake-baking mum, a Tressy doll that grew hair and a toy sink with proper plumbing – deserved our pity because she was rather 'cuddly', grew up slim and beautiful to marry a dentist like her Dad, whilst I was skinny and miserable and grew up – eventually – to be fat.

But when I was a child, loving sugar and wanting it became my *raison d'etre*. Not surprising then, that whenever I had money – like my weekly sixpence from Dad, or what I earned from running errands – I spent it on sweets. Straightaway. And one day my ship came in. I inherited a fortune. From little Mrs Bird, who lived on the corner of our road.

Or at least, I thought I had…

1966 Mrs Bird

'Where's the change?' said Mrs Bird.

'There isn't any.'

'Of course there is.'

'You told me to spend it.'

'What are you on about?'

'You said.'

I began to get the feeling that things were not quite right. I began to get that sinking feeling in the pit of my stomach, as I realised that I had made a mistake. I wished that I hadn't misunderstood her. I wished that I didn't have a paper bag stuffed with two shillings' worth of sweets bulging out from my fist. I hid the bag behind my back, squirmed uncomfortably and pulled at my lip.

'Where is it?' said Mrs Bird; diminutive old Mrs Bird; smaller than most people, smaller even than me and I was only eight years old.

'You said.' I stared down at the ground and scuffed the toe of one shoe in a wide circle. 'You said to buy something with the change.' I snatched a glance at her. 'So I did.'

Mrs Bird looked down at my toe, up at my face and then at the bag of sweets peeping out from behind my back.

'I see,' she said and threw her head back in a bitter gesture of acceptance; just as she had accepted long ago that she would never be tall, that she had foolishly married a man called Bird; and that though she had survived two world wars and a difficult life she had just been outwitted by an eight-year-old girl, who had come to cheat her out of her pension under the pretext of fetching her a packet of tea.

'You'd better get along then,' she snorted, 'and I shan't be asking you to go to the shop for me again.' As I stood there, not knowing what to do or how to put it right, her green front door with its lovingly polished brass knocker shut smartly in my scarlet face.

Only half an hour earlier I had been so happy; standing for ages and ages amongst the big glass jars of pink shrimps, peardrops, twisty cough-sweets and pineapple-chunks; the liquorice-sticks and sherbets; black-jacks, pink-jacks, the smarties and the chocolate buttons, trying to choose; gulping in all those delicious smells and knowing that I had two whole shillings to spend on penny sweets because she had told me to 'get something with the change'.

It was glorious, sublime, even. But I would have given it up in an instant if I could only have won back the high regard of Mrs Bird.

New Year 1998 The End of the Affair

It was just after Christmas. The children were out on a play date. I had a clear twenty minutes of free time to spend according to my whim. What a luxury. I could probably write the skeleton of a short story for my writers' circle in that time.

With my heart already singing in anticipation I tiptoed towards the back room door, intending to go left into the dining area, where my ancient Amstrad was set up and hummed a welcome to me.

But then the theme tune of a late afternoon soap suddenly blared out from the TV in the kitchen to the right.

Another possibility presented itself to me. I had a pack of

donuts in the cupboard that I was going to share with Mark and the kids after our evening meal.

So I could either write for twenty minutes, which would make me feel wholesome and comfortable and as if I had passed the time wisely, or...

... I could put my feet up in the kitchen, watch the daytime soap and eat my donut, which would make me feel guilty, greedy, useless and uncomfortable.

I stood in the doorway. I could see my computer on the left and the television on the right. Without knowing it, I stood, hesitating, at a major crossroads in my life.

I wanted to write. I really did. I took a step to the left. But somehow, seconds later, I found myself sitting on a kitchen chair in front of the TV, munching on a donut.

It was heaven. Sugar, fat and white flour all in one little round bundle of love. I had another. And another. And then thought I might as well eat all the evidence and throw the packaging away. The others would never even know.

Then I thought, would the children really remember that the rest of the chocolate tree decorations I had forgotten to put up were hidden somewhere in the kitchen? Had I even told them? No. I don't think they even knew about them. Yes!! Like Gollum searching for his precioussss I scrabbled in the back of the kitchen drawers until I'd liberated those little chocolate shapes. How annoying the wrappers were, they wouldn't come off, they were stuck fast though I scratched and scraped at them until, naked at last, the chocolate pieces leapt into my mouth and melted there, one after another until they were all gone and for a moment I was truly and gloriously happy.

And then... nothing. No more grub. Nothing left, except the hole inside me, yawning wider than ever. What I had eaten wasn't enough. Nothing – once I started on a sugar binge – was ever enough.

Then came the guilt, the shame and the self-disgust. What would people think if they saw me eating like that? What had I become?

And then something else. Something new.

The idea crept into my head that if I could make myself vomit, the food and guilt would go away as if it had never been. If I made a practise of that, I could eat whatever I wanted and still lose weight. The surgeon would agree to give me the hernia operation and I would be slim and beautiful again, like I was when I was young.

The compulsion to put my fingers down my throat was so strong it was almost overpowering. I curled my fingers around the seat of my chair and literally held myself in place, just managing to stop myself running to the bathroom.

In that moment when I physically clung to the chair, I had enough time to think about what I was contemplating. I knew what this was. It was called Bulimia. Princess Di had been talking about it. Everyone had been talking about it for years. I'd seen a Mike Leigh film about bulimia starring Jane Horrocks which had shocked me utterly.

I knew I was in the grip of insanity. I knew where the practise of purging would take me: towards even more compulsive behaviour and a horribly damaged body.

And in that moment I realised what was going on.

I wasn't eating the sugar. The sugar was eating me.

I had no chance of regulating my eating, because once I ate sugar I had no sensation of being full. There was never, ever, ever enough. One bite was too many. A thousand weren't enough.

Within a week I had found a support group for people with eating disorders and they confirmed what I already knew. I was an addict.

I had to admit that the sugar addiction that began with honey on my dummy when I was a baby was now running my life. I had to admit defeat. And admitting defeat was the end of the lifelong struggle. It was as if some giant hand (I'm naming no names) had lifted the roof from my house and called down to me to say, 'It's all right. You can come out now.'

I was ready to come out. I was ready to lose my weight. Finally.

On the advice of the group I stuck religiously to three meals a day with nothing in between and cut out my dear friend sugar altogether, because I knew I couldn't cut it down. I checked the contents of tins and packets and gave up sweet drinks and even alcohol, because of the sugar in it. And that also meant giving up cakes and donuts, biscuits and sweets, chocolate and ice-cream: all those foods that had given me so much joy for so long, and ultimately caused me so much grief.

At first I went into withdrawal and felt wretched, but I persisted and after three weeks the headaches stopped and I was free. I could dish up ice-cream and treats for the family and not feel anything at all. I didn't look back. I never deliberately ate sugar again, except once, when I had a short-lived affair with some Peking Duck wrapped in pancakes, where the sauce is almost pure sugar. It was delicious, but the next day my head felt like it was gripped in a giant vice and I was so ill I couldn't get out of bed. I knew that suddenly eating sugar again after a long break could have this effect but hadn't anticipated such a violent reaction. Not worth it, I decided.

Sugar became like someone I went out with once. Someone that got me into trouble, like Patsy Parkin.

Like another old friend, the sugar was gone. And good riddance.

Naughty, Naughty Belly-Breast!

Though it was nice to be slim and to see my plastic surgeon eating his hat as he hastily put me on his waiting list for the hernia operation, this dramatic weight loss created a new problem of asymmetry.

I had lost four stone over the course of a year, and my two breasts were now markedly different in size, the natural one having shrunk more drastically than the reconstruction.

I think it happened because the new breast was made up of muscle and fat from my stomach and no one had told it that it wasn't a stomach anymore. So it thought it still was. Stomach fat is trained to cling to us and make our lives a misery, whilst breast fat – the only fat we actually like – is always the first to go. It's Sod's Law innit?

Whatever the reason, I now had a real problem of asymmetry.

28 January 1999

Dear Mr C

I reviewed Mrs Day today. The result of the Free TRAM to the left breast remains good. Janice has lost a lot of weight and her problems now are asymmetry of the breasts, no nipple on the left side, muscle herniation and the abdominal scar. Janice is going to continue to lose some weight so in the first instance I am going to improve the muscle hernia with a mesh. At a later date when she has lost some further weight, I will then look at adjusting the shape and volume of the breasts.

Best wishes

Yours sincerely

Mr D

Consultant

The Outplant

As an answer to my problem of asymmetrical breasts I had taken to wearing a prosthesis inside my right bra-cup to plump out the natural breast so that it appeared as big as the left one. I felt permanently uncomfortable about the deception, fearing prosecution under the Trades Descriptions Act for impersonating a voluptuous woman. In truth, I felt as fake my falsie.

It was very hot to wear in the summer and also fell out sometimes when I bent over to pick something up, which was embarrassing. This is not a laughing matter. It reminded me of the poor woman who had accosted me the night before my operation and told me that her implant had fallen out onto her dinner plate. I felt the irony, keenly, that I had gone to all that trouble to have my new breast made from natural material and not from an implant, and yet here I was, wearing an implant on the outside.

It was, in fact, more of an out-plant.

These problems notwithstanding, I can honestly say that I was fond of my prosthesis. It was soft and warm and squishy. I liked to take it out, squeeze it and hold it against my cheek. Why should men and lesbians have all the fun with breasts, I reasoned, even false ones? I did try to remember not to do it in public though…

So we were friends, this squidgy creature and I, but there was no denying that it had a wayward personality. I eventually became so fed up with its behaviour that I began to think I might as well have it sewn inside the smaller, natural breast – or possibly another just like it, since it was getting a bit grubby – and sewn so firmly that it wouldn't fall out under any circumstances. This operation, a breast augmentation, is known in the vernacular as 'a boob job'.

First of all though, I needed a hernia repair. As I was already going into hospital to have that, I thought I might try and get my money's worth, so I asked to have another procedure done at the same time: some liposuction from the original, now oversized reconstruction. I was hoping in this way to sort out my asymmetry without having to have my outplant turned into an implant.

All of this obsession with how I looked was only partly driven by low self-esteem. It was also a neat diversion from my fear that the cancer might return.

28 September 1999
Seen in plastic surgery clinic Mr D, Consultant
Janice's weight is down to 10 stone now. It has meant a loss of
volume in her right breast, which is now smaller than the left,
but she is keen to leave well alone. The hernia on the right
side of the abdomen is very obvious, and this is going to need
mesh repair.

9 December 1999
Seen by co-operative doctor
Hernia op just over wk ago. 15 staples to be removed. Dr A

14 December 1999
Removal of clip from skin NEC. Removal of remaining clip
from hernia repair. Well healed. Sister N.

I'm sure that was true. It probably *was* 'well healed'. But
when I ran up the road after Michael, six weeks after my op,
I'm positive I felt something 'ping'. It could have been my
imagination of course, a similar experience to my hearing
hooves clatter across the roof and jingle bells in the sky when
I was eleven.

Which one of these experiences was true? Both? Neither?
It's a mystery.

6 February 2000
Seen in general surgery clinic by M, Reg to Mr D
Examination of the wounds today showed the scars have settled
well, and there is no evidence of recurrence of the hernia.

I have told Janice that the abdomen will be a rather strange shape because we have reinforced one area and hence the stomach may well bulge in the places where the mesh hasn't been laid. In addition to this the discomfort will persist because the mesh is there to induce scarring. I think she can now begin gentle exercises, such as swimming, and I told her to massage the scars as well.

She was worried about some dog ears on the left side of the abdomen where the scar was, but I have told her that we must let the scars settle now.

We shall review her in a year's time, to see whether she wishes anything further done here.

Desperately Seeking Symmetry

The hernia repair might have been a success – or so we all thought at the time – but the breast liposuction didn't work at all. My reconstructed breast looked exactly the same: still two cup sizes bigger than the other one.

I was much more concerned about the asymmetry in my breasts than I was about my bulging stomach. No matter how much it bulged, it still looked better than it had before I had the tummy tuck that had come on special offer with the original reconstruction. The failure of the breast liposuction, on the other hand, was a terrible blow. Mark repeatedly reassured me that it wasn't important but I couldn't let it go. It might not have been important to him, I said, but it was important to me.

I tried to tell myself that many women have uneven breasts. It didn't help. Mine had been even once and it just didn't feel right that they no longer were.

Of course my mania for symmetry was also tied up with other stuff.

Firstly, there was the obvious displacement activity of obsessing about my appearance in order to avoid the lingering anxieties about my illness. Then there was the default setting of low self-esteem that was set up for me in my earliest years, now coupled with the new crisis of going through a mastectomy, a traumatic surgical experience that attacked my body image at its core.

Or to put it more simply: I felt like a right tit.

1970 Feeling Like a Right Tit

Sofa-Jack, though he wasn't my first love, was definitely my greatest.

Inconveniently, at the time I fell for him I was going out with his friend Stephen Turner, whom I privately called the frog prince because he seemed like such a prince until the moment I first kissed him. Then he turned into a frog.

He stared at my mouth for a long time while he ran his tongue methodically all the way around his lips to drench them in spittle. Round and round. Nervously, I watched his lips get wetter and wetter. Then he leaned towards my face and the slow approach of those cold, wet, lips, glistening with drool, made my head stretch automatically backwards on my neck. I just couldn't help it.

But he came faster than I could elegantly recoil and before I knew it he was upon me. The kiss itself, however, was not fast. It was too wet for that. It slipped and slid slowly all over my mouth, or rather, the general area of my face where my mouth was located. It was pretty horrible; no, it was just horrible. There was nothing pretty about it.

But like any self-respecting teenage girl, I had to have a boyfriend, so I put up with it. Patsy was dating Stephen's friend Jack, and we would sit together on my mother's sofa in a line of four, snogging.

Gradually it emerged that Jack and I were more interested in each other than in our partners. I agonised about this terrible situation for some time, with me and Jack craning our necks to talk to each other and smile little secret smiles that our partners wouldn't see, until one day after a torrid session, Patsy confided in me that she really liked my boyfriend Stephen much more than she liked her boyfriend Jack.

I was astounded. How could she? I tried to see Jack through her eyes. It's true that he had terrible acne. He had so much acne he even had acne on top of his acne. And pointy teeth, like a werewolf. And hair like a brillo-pad. But he was big and smiley and one helluva guy, while Stephen was, frankly, a frog.

And glory be to God, it soon turned out that Patsy didn't mind Stephen's wet kisses at all. She confessed that she had a very dry mouth, so saliva of any kind was welcome. Even if it belonged to someone else.

No lawyers were involved, no pre-nuptial agreements or court hearings were necessary. We just informed the boys of the way things stood and swapped places on the sofa. Sorted. The kissing recommenced.

Very soon after that, Stephen chucked Patsy and asked me to come back to him. But I had Jack by then and he was seriously the big love of my young life, even though I don't remember doing anything at all with him other than sitting on my Mum's sofa and kissing.

I went out with Jack in this way for four whole weeks before he went away on a fortnight's holiday. It was a relationship of unheard-of longevity. As far as our peers were concerned, we were practically married.

But when he came back, he was funny with me. I don't mean to say that he was witty; in fact, he was rather dull. I resorted to thumping him in the genital area on a regular basis to entertain us when we weren't kissing.

And when we went to Annabel Edgar's birthday party, one of the very few and possibly the only occasion on which we emerged from my mother's sofa into the outside world, he avoided me altogether. I didn't see him until the end of the evening when he announced in front of goggle-eyed witnesses that he wanted to go out with Annabel Edgar from now on.

Sadly, it was perfectly understandable. That evening I was wearing a dress made of brown crimplene bought for me by my mother, which clung to me in lumpy brown clumps and made me look like an enormous truffle. What's more I was trying to grow out my fringe, so it was pulled back off my face with a row of Kirby grips and stood up from my head in a little frill, in the days when hair really wasn't supposed to do that.

It was a trauma of gigantic proportions. Jack delivered the news with grinning Annabel by his side and a hallway full of teenagers. All I could do was to say that I didn't want to go out with him anyway, though inside I was desolate.

'Good,' he said, and together they went back into the kissing room.

When I got home, oh horror of horrors, my Mum was in my bed. We had taken on a lodger and there weren't enough beds until my sister Jane left home.

I couldn't even cry until Mum was fast asleep and snoring loudly; and even then I still couldn't cry, because I had held in the tears for so long and so deeply that they had dried up into little tear-sized stones that couldn't get out. I only had a deep pain in my chest, because he really was the big love of my life, at the tender age of thirteen.

I carried a torch for Jack for nearly two years, watching him longingly from a distance and finding myself quite unable to get over him. He was big and ugly, acne-faced and pointy-toothed, dull and smiley and all mine for four whole weeks, until he ran off with the police commissioner's daughter.

Maybe that was one of the times in my life – one of many – when the tears that should have been cried turned into hard little lumps of pain inside my body and floated up and down my bloodstream, waiting for the day when they could cause the worst possible irritation and inconvenience by clustering together and forming a lump big enough to be called a cancer.

That might just be a silly idea. And then again, it might not.

The Writing on the Wall

In 2001, Mark and I were interviewed by a journalist friend for an article about good marriages in a national magazine. This came back to haunt us for years afterwards, whenever an acquaintance stumbled across an old copy in a doctor's surgery or a hairdresser's.

The idea was that we would be a shining example of a strong marriage. What a joke! I was no better at relationships than I had been at thirteen when I was thumping sofa-Jack in the genitals. However, I was up for it, since there was the chance of some free publicity photos of me afterwards – if I smiled prettily at the photographer – so I dragged poor private Mark along with me, despite his violent protests.

I told the journalist about our method of using a 'talking stick' to facilitate better communication; the idea being that whoever holds the stick gets to speak without interruption. I smiled sadly to myself when I read the printed article and saw the truth between the lines. We needed a talking stick because we couldn't communicate without one, and if it had been any bigger I would probably have hit him over the head with it.

Then I was quoted saying that 'if it weren't for the children we would have split up years ago', to which Mark retorted, 'but if it weren't for the children we would have a relationship.'

Our caustic quips made excellent copy for the mag and the delighted photographer snapped us snuggling on the sofa. We were, at least, always good at snuggling on sofas.

Of course, Mark hadn't intended to say that he regretted having the children. He was a great father in many ways, especially when they were small, but despite sounding and looking like a great big comfy bear, inside he had that difficult combination of vulnerability and pride, so that he could neither cope with life on his own, nor allow himself to ask for help when he needed it. And that was difficult to live with.

We always had these problems with communication but our long talking-stick sessions usually managed to bring things around. Sex helped, which was good between us when we got round to it, and so did our infrequent weekends away from the kids. We would rediscover the fun of being together; fun that had somehow got lost in the struggle to bring up children, pay the bills and survive the cancer.

I had also read somewhere that couples should never go to sleep on a quarrel, which I believed gave me *carte blanche* to harangue Mark far into the night whenever we disagreed, until he came around to my way of thinking. I think I would have made a good torturer. I have missed my vocation.

When the periods of non-communication stretched into weeks, I dragged him by the hair to marriage guidance counselling. The first of these sorties had the magical effect of bringing us back together again straight away. We were so united in our dislike of that particular counsellor that we agreed we didn't need to go back there ever again, and walked home, holding hands for the first time in ages.

While we were still selfish children, playing at life before our own children came along and catapulted us into maturity, our relationship worked very well. There was plenty wrong with him, but there were many things right with him too. Handsome and strong, broad-shouldered and cuddly, for a while in the early years he held me in place and made me feel safe.

But when things started to go wrong I became increasingly convinced – with my love of labels – that there was something else going on; something like Asperger's, or narcissistic personality disorder, or arrested emotional development; or something for which there isn't actually a label that might explain why he was incapable of articulating his feelings or communicating his needs; or just a great big pudding that stopped loving me and tried to pretend that it didn't matter.

But it did matter. It mattered to me.

Of course, I played no part in the failure of our relationship. I didn't decide that I could get enormously fat and wear threadbare leggings and no make-up for ten years because I was 'a Mum'; and I didn't turn into a shrieking, bitter harridan because he 'wasn't the man I thought I had married.' No sir. Not I.

Well all right then, maybe I did. A bit.

They say that marriages fail because women think that men will change and they don't; whereas men think that women will not change and they do. And I fear that's true, at least in our case.

The writing was on the wall for us and I could see it. I pointed it out to him, often, but he wouldn't listen. On the occasions when he hurt me and wouldn't apologise I said that little by little he was killing my love for him; that one day it would all be gone, and – worst of all – I wouldn't care. That's what frightened me. Not the pain, but the faint stirrings of indifference.

He had his own ideas. 'You're just insecure because of your parents' divorce,' he would say. 'You're trying to push me away to see if I will go, and I won't. Don't worry. I won't leave you.'

But he was wrong. We really were in trouble. I was falling out of love with him, year after year. With every hurtful word and forgotten promise I could feel the love slipping away from me; but like the little child who cried wolf I had lost my right to be heard. So I would give up trying to address our problems and submit to a cuddle, not only because I couldn't get through to him, but because I wanted so much to believe, as he did, that nothing was wrong.

And I was also busy. Busy staying alive.

The Words of the Wise Woman

The wise woman said that if I did not change the environment in which the cancer thrives, no matter how effectively I destroyed it, it would return. The wise woman said, in effect, that I needed to change.

So I did. I changed what I ate and thus how I looked. And I changed what I did and thus how I felt.

But – being far from perfect – there were some things I failed utterly to change.

I tried to give up anti-perspirant deodorants because they apparently contain aluminium which is thought to be very bad for you. But when I used the non-anti-perspirant kind, I got sweaty. I didn't like that. There's an old saying: women glow, men perspire and horses sweat. I am not a horse.

I tried to give up non-organic vegetables, so I began to have organic ones delivered, but the ones I ordered came straight from the field, covered in dirt. I decided that I didn't want to spend any part of my possibly shortened life scrubbing potatoes. I would rather eat genetically modified vegetables that look nice and kill me.

I also tried to worry about the household products that contain vicious carcinogens. So should we all, although we shouldn't worry too much, since worrying is bad.

Thus I could not advance to my shiny new healthy lifestyle without worrying and stressing, and I could not retreat from it without deciding not to care about what I ate or what products I bought.

It was all very worrying. And I wasn't supposed to do that.

So I just quietly tried to buy the healthy products with no damaging chemicals and eat more vegetables and take vitamins. And I did change. I really did. I had regular healing, lost tons of weight, did tai chi and homeopathy and had massages and drank hot water.

Giving up stuff was easier than remembering to behave differently. I found goal-setting fun as long as I didn't take failure too seriously. All I needed to do was try again and keep on trying until I got it.

I guess that doing stuff I shouldn't be doing and eventually giving it up because it's making my life a misery has always been a hobby of mine. And when I'm bored with that I suppose I might, in the end, give up giving-up-stuff and just stand still.

But not yet.

Stressy Tessy

The thing I absolutely needed to give up and with which I struggled the most was stress.

But I was on to it in a big way. Since first getting my diagnosis of cancer, no one had fussed, fretted and stressed themselves out more completely than I had about the danger of fussing, fretting and stressing oneself out.

I knew I had to stop; to change from being a human-doing

to a human-being; to replace constant working and busyness with the four 'R's: Rest, Relaxation, Recreation and Recovery.

All this I knew. It was perfectly clear that if I was going to survive I urgently needed to follow the advice of the wise woman and change from being a Type A personality (crazy) into a Type B personality (calm and centred). I needed to calm down and there wasn't a moment to lose.

I yelled at myself: 'Be calm! Be serene! And be quick about it!'

Yet I steadfastly ignored the voice that whispered to me that Mark was the greatest cause of stress in my life; that the presence of Mark, if anything, had to go.

But I had to balance the stress of having him around against the stress of breaking up the family, especially when the children were small and I was in and out of hospital. How would that help any of us?

Another idea kept me in the relationship. It was the thought that no other man in his right mind would ever want me now that I was damaged goods. And I was not just damaged by the breast cancer. I was damaged by the marriage. My confidence had been gradually eroded over the years, and like many people in a broken relationship, I suffered from the growing idea that there was something horribly wrong with me because we had not been able to keep on loving one another.

Then something happened. His parents split up and two unhappy people quickly became four happy ones. I saw that and wanted it too. Why shouldn't I find love again? And with my shortened life expectancy, how could I stay in an unhappy marriage even for a minute?

A woman I knew had recently chucked out her husband

and seemed suddenly to come alive. I asked her how she found the courage to do it. 'You will, when you're ready,' she said. I shook my head. I wasn't ready yet.

An older friend found me crying after a bitter argument with Mark. She said I shouldn't worry about it now; I should go when I could walk away. Not understanding, I asked her what she meant.

'One day,' she said, 'I woke up, swung my legs out of the bed and said to myself, 'Today's the day I go and see the solicitor. And it was as easy as that.'

I listened. I learned. I watched and waited. I wondered if it was the cancer that had brought my marriage down. Or was the opposite true? If it hadn't been for the illness that bonded us in adversity for a while, would we have split up years before?

I couldn't answer that. I just gave up trying to warn him and let the ties that bound us loosen; slowly, slowly, one by one.

Getting Abreast of it

Meanwhile I still struggled to look 'normal', though what normal was, I really had no idea. I couldn't shrink the reconstruction, so I thought perhaps I could have the natural breast made bigger. The surgeon had offered this a couple of times but I had always rejected the idea, not wanting an implant.

However, once I had accepted the idea that I already had an 'outplant' I began to see an 'augmentation' as a real possibility for me.

5 February 2002
Seen in plastic surgery clinic by O, Registrar
Your patient returned to clinic for further review. It is now
six years since we carried out a left breast free TRAM
reconstruction. There had been right abdominal herniation
over the subsequent years and she had mesh repair carried out
in 1999.

At present her main problems are related to asymmetry. She
feels the right breast is too small and therefore uses an insert to
try and achieve symmetry within a bra. Her second problem
is that the hernia seems to have recurred. Her third problem is
that the lateral dog ears of the abdominal scars have persisted.

I discussed a number of surgical options with her today. As
far as the breast asymmetry is concerned, I suggested that the
easiest way to solve this problem would be to insert a silicone
breast implant under the right breast.

She would need approximately 150-200ml. I have outlined
the risk of the procedure and the risks related to the implant.

As far as the hernia is concerned, this is really not a hernia,
but more lower abdominal weakness, and I have warned her
that re-exploration may not improve the situation. If she
decided to go ahead with any or all these procedures, then
we could also deal with the dog ears on her abdominal scar.
I suggested she should go away and think about things, and
return to the clinic in one week for further discussions before
we add her name to our waiting list.

When I came back the following week, I said that I would like
to go on Mr D's waiting list for a breast augmentation.

A Dab Hand at Hernias

I was still visiting Mr C from time to time so that he could see I was still alive. He would call me back into the hospital, say 'Are you still alive?' and when I said, 'Yes, barely,' he would say, 'Good' and put a tick by my name on the list of people whose lives he had saved. And for a few months, that would be that.

Since Mr C was also rumoured to be a dab hand at hernias, on one visit I decided to ask him about mine. The area was still sticking out and hurting when I coughed or sneezed. The previous op, in my opinion, hadn't really worked. I confessed that I had chased Michael up the street only six weeks afterwards, when I'd felt the 'ping'. Maybe the mesh had become detached at one end and rolled up into a little ball, like a T-shirt riding up under a cardigan?

Mr C said he didn't see how my chasing Michael would have been a problem. I think they have a policy in the NHS of denying the patient's notions of culpability for their illness, so that if you say 'Was this my fault?' they always say 'No.'

I like that policy. It's a good one. And thankfully, my kids have adopted it too.

Denying Mum's Culpability

Michael, when he was little, was quite simply a devil on legs.

Abbie, on the other hand was a little angel, perfect in every way. Abbie on the naughty chair was such an unusual sight I had to take a photo of her or we would never have believed it had happened. Of course she was only playing along with us, biding her time until, with the coming of her teens, her latent demonic tendencies could flower.

But when they were children, Michael was the one that gave me all the trouble. He was what parents in the know call 'a runner', which means that he ran away at every opportunity. It got so bad that for a time I kept him on a leash. I had to, otherwise he would just go. And he delighted in the furore this caused. One time he slammed the front door so I'd think he had run away, which of course I did; and when I came back, demented from running around the streets looking for him, I found him grinning behind the sofa.

He started this practise of running away as soon as he could walk. When he was only a tiny tot I took him up to the Downs where the ground is clear and flat for miles and let him go, to find out if he would really leave me, hoping to prove the psychologists' theory that a child will not abandon its mother. But Michael did. Off he went. And not looking back once, he just kept going.

He did it because he wanted to be free, out in the open air, on his own. Just like his Mum.

A deep thinker from a very early age, Michael confronted the world head-on and made his own sense of it. Catching sight of my nipple-less breast one day when he was only five, he clapped his chubby little hand to his forehead and said:

'Now I know why you don't have a nibble, mummy!'

'Do you?' I said. 'Why's that then?'

'So you'll know which boobie is the poorly one.'

Dagnabbit, I knew there was a reason!

And what's more, it makes a lot of sense to call them nibbles...

The children tell me now that they don't remember the time

when I had cancer, and I hope that's because it hasn't damaged them. But as well as my mistake in sending them away while I had the operation, there was one aspect of the fallout that must have affected them even if they don't realise it...

After the operation I was advised not pick up anything heavy because of the danger of lymphodaema in my left arm. This advice was born out by my arm's behaviour. In the early years it would swell up with very little provocation and was difficult to deflate. The children were sturdy creatures, and heavy, so when I came out of hospital, even after I had healed up, I was never able to pick them up again.

That must surely have affected them, especially Abbie. It's harsh not to be picked up by your mother when you are only three.

But apart from the unavoidable knowledge that mummy was not allowed to pick things up, even them, and that she had a poorly boobie – clearly marked by the absence of a nibble – I deliberately kept away from them any notion that I might die, or even that I was ill; and I refused the chemotherapy with their well-being partly in mind.

I didn't want them to know that I was anywhere near death. I wanted their childhood to feel safe in ways that mine never had.

So they tell me they don't remember any of it. And I choose to believe them.

Good Works

'Macduff was from his mother's womb untimely ripped'

Like Macduff, I had ripped myself untimely from the loving embrace of the NHS and told them where to put their nasty medicine. But beneath my bravado, I was feeling pretty scared about my decision and wondering whether I could survive on my own. No one could reassure me about that either. Yes, I was doing well, but my survival was by no means guaranteed.

Certainly no insurance company was willing to take a chance on me, which did nothing for my confidence.

I decided to turn my attention to the great risk assessor in the sky, the Good Lord Almighty. The wise woman had told me that God would surely not gather to His bosom any one of His children that was not making herself useful. I considered this idea carefully. Was I really making myself useful? As an entertainer, perhaps. But that was a fairly subjective idea and my confidence in myself as an entertainer fluctuated on a daily basis. As a mother, clearly not, since my deficiencies in that area were as plain to see as Michael's latest escapade.

What about good works in the Parish? What about taking a basket of fruit around to the worthy poor?

It was an idea, until I remembered that in this particular Parish there weren't many people poorer or more worthy of charity than I was myself; and buying myself a basket of fruit was probably not what God had in mind.

'What about fund-raising?' said the voice.

I threw myself on my knees and prayed fervently.

'Spare me, Oh Great White Spirit,' I begged. 'Not fund-raising! Anything but that.'

1967 Rubbish Works

One day in the long hot summer between primary and secondary school, Suze and Patsy Parkin eagerly agreed when I proposed that we three should stage an outdoor play on the grassy roundabout outside my house. Our plan was to charge tuppence for the seats and give the proceeds to charity.

The play was to be a simple affair with no story. We would simply make one up as we went along.

We put up a small tent on the roundabout. We set out some kitchen chairs. I had my recorder. We may even have had a sketchy plot. I feel sure we did, but it's lost to me now.

All we needed was an audience.

We consulted my Mum. She suggested that we knock on the door of every house on the estate and advertise our play.

We executed this excellent plan and although no one actually promised to come, several neighbours proffered donations along with words of praise for our endeavour.

On the way round we picked up a small boy whose mother wanted rid of him for a few hours. She sent him with money, to pay for his seat in the auditorium.

Alas, he also brought along a copy of The Beano and didn't take his nose out of it for the entire performance, much to our chagrin, since he was the only attendee.

Even my Mum, despite prolonged entreaties from all three of us, said she was too busy to come.

'People will turn up once you've started,' she said.

Dispirited, we began our play, or rather I began it, with some incidental music played on my recorder. After a few minutes there were complaints from the other cast members. They said the incidental music was going on for too long and was also rubbish.

I retreated into the tent and played on. I was putting off the moment when I was going to have to produce a script, or at the very least a vague storyline.

Patsy came into the tent and tried to rip the recorder from my tender lips, much to my fury. I retaliated by wrestling her to the ground. After a few seconds the tent pole was knocked down and we were lost in the collapsed canvas.

It was some time before we emerged, only to see Suze's stiff little back disappearing into the distance. The small boy spoke at last.

'That girl says you're really stupid and she's going home.'

We felt that the whole episode had been an unmitigated disaster, until we looked in the collection pot and found the amazing sum of three shillings and sixpence.

We decided to give it to the local old folks' day centre and took it down there straight away. Thrusting it into the hands of one of the nurses, we informed her that it was the takings from the performance of our outdoor play that very afternoon. She was delighted, and made me give her my name and address.

We thought that was the end of it and could only congratulate ourselves on the lucky escape we had experienced, there having been no witnesses to our awful apology for a play – aside from the small boy who had not looked up from his comic.

A few days later, however, we received a letter of thanks from the Matron of the Day Centre, along with a request for us to perform our play for the old people at our earliest convenience. They were all looking forward to seeing our play very much, the letter said.

We were horrified. We couldn't understand why God was punishing us in this way for what was, after all, a simple good deed.

It was left up to me to get us off the hook, as I was the originator of this non-play and largely responsible for its failure on account of my rogue recorder playing.

I was sick with fear as I stood before the kindly Matron. I hung my head, beetroot-faced, and had to be asked to speak up several times.

'We can't do the play,' I stammered eventually.

'But why not, dear?' said the Matron. 'We'd love to see it.'

'It's not very good,' I said. 'It's kind of... rubbish.'

'Oh, come along, I'm sure it's wonderful.'

'No, it... there aren't any lines, or any parts, or...' I sneaked a glance up at her increasingly bewildered face and rushed for the climax, 'any story.'

There. It was said. I stared hard at the floor and waited to be told off.

'Oh.' She sounded disappointed and puzzled, but she rallied. 'Well, never mind dear. It's the thought that counts.'

I gazed up at her wonderingly. It was true then. It was, after all, the thought that counted.

What a relief.

The Laying-On of Hands

Since that first disastrous attempt at fund-raising for the old folks' day-centre in 1967, I had not tried again. In truth, I simply didn't understand the fund-raising thing. Why would anybody want to spend their spare time in some physically harmful, often ridiculous and invariably humiliating activity in order to raise a few quid when they could easily write a cheque for the same amount and not have to do the bungee jump or fifty-mile hike in their underwear?

I looked for a different path into God's good books.

After some reflection I remembered Jesus. He was clearly a nice person. If I couldn't get my head around fund-raising, I could certainly get my head around being nice to people.

Having been influenced by my mother's beliefs, the form of selflessness with which I was most familiar was the kind I found in the spiritualist churches.

There is no nicer bunch of people than the spiritual healers, I thought. God must love them to bits.

I had attended regular sessions with the National Federation of Spiritual Healers since coming out of hospital and was firmly convinced that healing had been instrumental in my survival. It occurred to me that maybe I could help others in the same way. After serious consideration I decided to become a spiritual healer myself.

What a stroke of luck that I was the progeny of a long line of old-style spiritualists! Taught by her own mother, my Mum had been giving healing to people since she was sixteen years old. With reverent tones, I asked her to share her wisdom with me.

She thought long and hard before offering some very helpful advice.

'Well, there's one thing you ought to know,' she said. 'If you find yourself needing to give healing to a person's private parts...'

'Pardon?' I said, alarmed.

'It can happen.'

'Ok.'

'You just take their hand and lay it on their private part for them, and then you put your hand on top of theirs. See?'

'Oh. Right…'

She nodded, happy in the knowledge that her daughter could now go out into the world as a healer and not wreak havoc; happy that I was now unlikely to disgrace the healing fraternity with any unwise laying-on of hands.

1970 Penis Adventures and the Butcher's Etchings

By the time I was thirteen, things had begun to hot up. Jack had broken my heart, but in time it healed and was stolen by a new seducer. A disreputable boy. A heartbreaker, with an exquisite face, long, long lashes around his baby blue eyes and a glamorous profession: he was a butcher's apprentice.

Even at the age of sixteen he was a player and seduced me with practised ease, until one day he decided the time was ripe to bestow on me the gift of carnal knowledge, so he invited me to put my hand down his trousers and feel 'that.'

I demurred, several times, until he grabbed said hand and guided it into the delightful world of his underpants.

There was a large, living, pulsating creature in there, not like anything I had ever felt before. It was a tall cylindrical thing and had the quality of being very hard, as if it were made of rubber, whilst at the same time having a soft layer of skin covering the hardness; and that thin layer seemed to move a little under my touch.

It was unlike anything I had ever felt before in my life, and I wasn't sure if it was nice.

I stood there, while he held my wrist inside his trousers, not knowing what was expected of me, until I eventually curled my fingers around it and for a few seconds gripped it with all my might before snatching my hand out and shrieking as if I'd touched a spider.

That was my first encounter with the beast that rises in the night. The second came soon after.

On our next date he formally invited me to see his etchings. He came to pick me up at our house, and when we had finally escaped from my mother's questioning, which was a bit like the vicar's wedding interview, we set out on our adventure.

We walked for a long time, long enough for us to get to know each other well. I sang for him, a folk song called 'Black is the colour of my true love's hair', and I believed that he was in love with me when he told me so. And I believed that I was in love with him.

When we arrived at a large deserted mansion on the other side of town, I willingly accepted his story that he knew the owners. My true love wouldn't lie to me, surely? He climbed over the wall and I waited at the front door for him to appear and let me in.

He led me upstairs to the ballroom, a huge room with floor-to-ceiling mirrors and a practice barre, and when he started to kiss me in the moonlight it all seemed terribly right and romantic, even when my trousers slid mysteriously to my ankles. His suggestion that we lie down seemed like a good idea too.

But then I felt something that I didn't understand. Terrified, I screamed and pushed him off me. I pulled up my trousers while *he lay amazed on the floor, and I ran away, out of the room and down the stairs, over the wall around the house, along the road, into the field behind the houses and down, down, down the grassy slope past the hollow lightning-blasted oak tree where I had often played as a child.*

I ran from the danger as fast as I could, and didn't stop when I heard him calling my name from a great distance away. I only ran, and didn't stop running until I was home, which was a good two miles. That's how afraid I was.

I did see that boy again – he even served me drinks at the youth club – but we avoided each other's eyes, and I never told anyone what happened, not even my friends. What he thought of me I'll never know, but I was definitely very afraid of him.

And the thing that had made me so afraid and so confused? It was that creature again, pushing between my legs, pushing and pushing until it started to hurt a lot, and I could feel the strangeness of it; that thing that has its own life and yet is not sentient; the thing that is hard and at the same time silky; is stiff and yet bends; and most of all, is attached to another human being's body, whereas it isn't anywhere, not anywhere at all, attached to mine.

The Abominable Abdominal Wall

18 March 2002
Seen in general surgery clinic, by Mr C, Consultant
I am sorry to hear Janice has had problems following repair of her incisional hernia. She says this has been present ever since the surgery was done.

She is aware of this fullness of the lateral end of the

scar which is painful on coughing. She is also aware of the mesh under the right subcostal margin.

Clinically there is a fullness at the lateral end of the scar but I could not convince myself of a definite cough impulse. It is possible to feel the mesh in the upper abdomen and I suspect this may well have separated from where it was sutured and it does feel as though it has rolled up. This can sometimes occur.

I thought in order to elucidate this further it would be helpful to get a CT scan of her abdominal wall which I have arranged. I will see her with the results and then we can discuss it further.

22 August 2002
Seen in general surgery clinic by Mr C, Consultant
Janice has now had her CT which does show there is a defect lateral to the mesh you placed for her incisional hernia repair. This is most prominent when she stands, giving her some discomfort. I have recommended that it would be worth exploring with a view to repair, but warned her that there is always a risk of further recurrence.

One couldn't help thinking, at this stage, that if only one hadn't been so stubborn in the first place and gone for the more straightforward operation of using the Latisimuss Dorsi muscle from the back and not the Rectus Abdominis from the tummy-tum-tum, one wouldn't have ended up in such a pickle. But when did one ever do the sensible thing?

The months rolled by and I got on with my ordinary life as best I could.

No Sex Please, I have a Morbid Fear of Sperm

I was working for the NHS myself by this time, temping in the local hospital's psychiatric ward, which felt like my true spiritual home. I worked part-time and tried to write this book on my days off.

But there was something rotten in the State of Denmark; or anyway, if not Denmark, there was certainly something rotten in the state of our marriage. I tried once more to put it right. Sex-wise.

With my usual love of melodrama, I decided that my diminishing libido was the result of a morbid fear of sperm. Perhaps I wasn't thinking altogether clearly, but I did know that I had gone off sex to the point of repulsion and I also knew that I needed help.

I remember my GP's rather-too-careful reaction to the news. It was that look again; the 'Where's the panic button in case I need it' look that I have come to expect from the medical fraternity.

'What gives you that idea?' he said.

'I can't bear my husband's bodily fluids,' I said. 'First it was sperm, then it became sweat and now it's even his saliva. It's not normal.'

When he had recovered, he asked me what I'd like to do about it.

'I want to see someone. Someone who knows about sex.'

'You mean you want to be referred to a psychosexual counsellor?'

'Yes,' I said. 'One of those.'

I wasn't just attention-seeking; I was trying once more

to save my marriage. I couldn't get Mark to talk about our failing sex life, which had once been so good. Sex had been a great way for us to smooth over the rough patches in the early years. The intimacy of it brought us back from the cold places and bonded us again in love and warmth. Well, it did for me anyway. Without it, the rift was widening almost daily. I wanted to believe Mark when he said my scars and nipple-less breast didn't matter. But maybe it did. Maybe the idea that it mattered was putting me off. I wasn't sure. I only knew that I had a growing revulsion to the idea of sex.

The doctor explained in medic-speak that what I was asking for was a bit of a to-do.

'It will mean a tertiary referral,' he said.

'What's that,' I said, having foolishly chosen to study German at school rather than Latin, and then got thrown out of German anyway, for being disruptive.

'You'll have to be seen by three people. I'll be the first; then you'll have to have a psychiatric assessment and then an assessment by the psychosexual counsellor.'

'Sounds good,' I said. Not exactly the reaction he was hoping for, but he went ahead and referred me to a psychiatrist to discuss the possibility.

In the event this caused a minor hullabaloo, since the psychiatrist in question worked in the very same psychiatric department that was currently employing me as a temp. When they found out, my fellow secretaries worried they might be called upon to type up my notes. Questions of confidentiality were raised.

I decided to resolve the situation by facing it head on.

I called the main players together for a meeting – the head of admin, the secretaries and one of the other psychiatric Consultants – and sat them in a circle. Then I leaned forward to speak in a hushed voice, which prompted them all to lean forward too.

'I know some of you are concerned about a possible breach of confidentiality,' I began.

They nodded, solemnly.

'So,' I went on, 'I thought the best way forward would be to tell you what's going on, so then it won't be confidential any more. And if it's not confidential then the confidentiality can't be breached, can it?'

While they grappled with that I went for the kill.

'I need this appointment so I can be referred to a psycho-sexual counsellor, on account of the fact that I have developed a morbid fear of sperm.'

After a second or two of stunned silence, everybody looked to the Consultant for a final arbitration in the affair. He thought carefully about it, and then said that as it was only a one-off, and as one of the secretaries had volunteered to type up the notes, and as I had promised to keep my nose out of my own file if I should stumble across it in the filing cabinet, we would say no more about it.

We were all very relieved and went our separate ways. And, strangely, it improved my relationships with everyone involved. Communication always does. Or to put it another way, things are better out than in.

1971 Better Out than In

One night I was standing on my own at a party when some loutish lad molested me from behind. Never backward in coming forward, as my old Mum would say, I hurled my pint of cider over his head and instantly became the life and soul of the party, getting all the attention and carrying off the prize at the end of the night, in the form of Sean Murphy, the handsomest boy in the room. In fact, it was a commonly held belief that Sean Murphy was the handsomest boy in town; nay, in the country; in fact, in the universe. So by becoming his consort, I was made. My cool rating amongst my peers – with regard to boys anyway – was henceforward to be permanently off the scale.

Sean was not just handsome, he was heaven. He wrote poetry. He was the cleverest boy in his year. And he lived in a big rambling country house with a Mum and Dad who loved each other, and had siblings who were also beautiful and talented. He was a real prince. To me he was the epitome of the alpha male.

He had a paper-round for which he used one of those wonderful old bikes with the iron carry-basket up front. I would put on my best floaty, romantic dress; he would lift me up into the basket and cycle away with me. I felt like a damsel on a white charger.

Sean had genteel parents who listened to Radio 4 and watched BBC2 and he would sit me down for hours to listen to classical music until I could identify all six of the Bach Brandenburg Concertos. Then he'd flash art postcards at me, hundreds of them, until I knew the names of all the paintings and their painters. If I had any sort of education, it was at Sean's hands, not my school's.

When the boys' school imported us girls to play the female

parts in their latest Shakespearian production, it was sweet and
fitting that I should play Ophelia to his Hamlet.

I was so much in love with Sean that I only held out against
his ardour for six months and finally lost my cherry to him one
Saturday afternoon when we were alone in the house, gladly
giving up my virginity and not finding the pain at all tiresome
or terrifying. And afterwards, because I loved him, I jumped
up and down without protest at his request, so that the sperm
he had recklessly bestowed upon me would not fertilise my egg.
For what sperm could possibly manage the long swim upstream,
when the girl was jumping up and down?

Like I said, things are better out than in.

No Sex Please... but Why?

The assessment with the psychiatrist had gone well. Even
though she had clearly thought there was nothing wrong with
me, she agreed to the referral and I was put on the waiting list
for a psychosexual counsellor.

I waited another six months until the appointment arrived,
and at the final hour Mark decided he wasn't going to go
through with it. Typically, even though he'd agreed to the
project in the first place, when push came to shove, he just
wouldn't come.

'I don't have a problem with our sex life,' he said. 'You do.'
I pointed out to him that if I had a problem then we both had
a problem, but he wouldn't budge.

So I had to go on my own, only to have my opinion that
we were in this mess together confirmed. The counsellor told
me that there wasn't really very much point in going ahead

without Mark, although she was happy to try.

'You're preaching to the converted,' I said.

When I got home I told Mark what she had said, but he was unimpressed and still refused to come.

In the second session the counsellor nailed it, right fair and square, directly on the head.

Something that had been troubling me for a couple of months, I said. In the heat of an argument Mark had accused me of being frigid, and claimed that this was the cause of my growing aversion to sex. In the past, disappointed young men had called me all sorts of things. Several had diagnosed me as a lesbian, and others terrified me with accusations that I would be responsible for their aching and swollen balls dropping off in the night if I didn't agree to sleep with them. But no one had ever called me frigid – and this was my husband, with whom I had lived for many years. I wondered if the cancer experience had affected me more badly than I had realised. For the sake of my marriage, I thought I'd better get it sorted. And that was why I was sitting in her office talking about my morbid fear of sperm.

She nodded.

But, here's the funny thing, I said. During the six months when I was on her waiting list, I'd found myself strongly attracted to a married friend of mine. It wasn't his fault that I pursued him and he did an excellent job of turning me down, so it was really nothing. But the point was... I didn't feel repulsed by him. Au contraire, I felt aroused. So, if I really had developed a phobia of male bodily fluids, how could that be something that came and went? I was genuinely confused.

'Well, douche-ball,' she said (or perhaps something a little less rude than that, but that was the gist).

'Sorry?' I said.

'You felt aroused by this other man because you fancied him.'

'I fancied him?' I stared at her, amazed by the simple-mindedness of her answer, and thinking, 'Is this the sort of insightful wisdom you develop after years of study and with an impressive title like psychosexual counsellor on your door?'

She went on. 'And you don't want to have sex with your husband because you don't.'

'I don't what?'

'You don't fancy your husband.'

So there it was in black and white, the thing that I had been denying for months, maybe even years. I didn't want to have sex with Mark because I didn't fancy him. It wasn't due to some rare psychiatric condition after all. It was a simple case of 'gone-off-ness'.

'And if he won't come to these sessions,' she went on, 'there's very little chance of us doing anything about it.'

I agreed, and neither of us could see any point in my coming again. We said our goodbyes and I left, never to return; and whilst I was happy to hear that I wasn't frigid after all, I was also sad, very sad, to know that the nail she had hit so firmly on the head, was another nail in the coffin for Mark and me.

Still Alive Then?

28 November 2001
Seen in breast clinic by Mr C, Consultant
Further to previous correspondence, I saw Janice again today.
This was for her breast cancer follow-up. There are certainly no
features of concern in her right breast and the reconstructed
left breast is satisfactory.

She has declined a mammogram and I have therefore
recommended an ultrasound for assessment of the right
breast.

She has mentioned that she would like to have an
augmentation of the right breast and she is going to discuss
this further with Mr D.

I will see her in 12 months for a follow-up with regard to
her breast cancer. As you know she is on my waiting list for
repair of an incisional hernia.

Still alive then? The question hung in the air between us and
we were both happy to see it there. He ticked me off on his
clipboard, and home I went.

I had begun to hate those check-ups. One excellent spin-
off from having a life-threatening disease was that it cured
my hypochondria: by this time I'd had enough of doctors and
hospitals to last me a lifetime.

Alas, this didn't deter me from trying to get my breasts
the same size. It had become an obsession, a distraction from
my fear of dying and a desperate attempt not to live up to my
mother's description of my entry into the world as a B-movie
monster. All of which, of course, might have been avoided

if only I'd taken my Maverick friend Val's advice and had a double mastectomy at the time of my original operation.

One natural breast, with sensation in the nipple: worth a little lop-sidedness? Perhaps. But by this time, what with the hernia saga and unhappy in my marriage, I had lost the plot.

Putting the Cherry on the Trifle

Not only was I still obsessed with my divergent cup sizes, I was also painfully aware that in the nipple arena I was one short of a pair.

I thought, if I'm going back in anyway, maybe I should get a job-lot done and have a nipple made too? I'd never really been attracted to the idea of a surgically reconstructed nipple, being under the impression that it had to come from parts of me that I didn't want the surgeon's knife to reach. But I discovered by chance that it was possible to have a fake nipple, made of silicone. And someone I knew said she knew someone who knew someone who apparently had 'a fantastic one'.

I was excited. I tracked down the woman with the stick-on nipple and spoke to her on the phone. She sang its praises and told me that she had two models: one that was erect and one that wasn't. So she had one for every occasion, as it were.

I wondered whether, in the height of passion, she would suddenly say, 'Excuse me, kind sir, I just have to change my nipple, to better demonstrate my arousal'?

I decided not to ask her, and she promised to send me one of her spares so that I could examine it at my leisure. I could hardly wait, hawkishly watching the doormat every morning until it arrived.

I ripped the package open like a child at Christmas, and pulled out the nipple. It was amazing. I rolled up my sleeve and put it on my bare arm and it really looked as if there was a nipple growing there, for no reason whatsoever.

Later that day I went out for a meal with my girlfriends. Thinking to raise a laugh in the restaurant, I laid the nipple on my forearm and casually stretched my hand out across the table.

The first one to notice it screamed loudly and waved a shaking finger. 'My God,' she said, 'what's happened to your arm!'

Shrieks all round were followed by shouts of laughter when they realised the joke.

What larks we had with that poor lady's private part!

Contrite, I sent it back to her with thanks and determined to get one of my own. I begged my GP to refer me to the hospital that had produced it. After a while the referral came though and off I went, hope, as usual, singing in my heart.

On arrival, the surgeon asked me to drop my trousers, as surgeons often do. He wanted to see my hernia, which had reappeared following the first repair. Staring straight ahead, I obligingly dropped them to my knees. To my surprise the Consultant, nurse and senior house officer all looked a little shocked. Surely it wasn't *that* disgusting?

I looked down and was horrified to see that I had come out in a pair of Mark's boxer shorts.

I stammered an apology for the fact that I was wearing my husband's knickers. It was something about being behind with the laundry. The Consultant said he supposed it was marginally better than the other way round. The SHO began giggling hysterically at this and couldn't stop throughout the whole consultation, which we all found rather irritating.

But that was the end of the jollity for me. The Consultant went on to deliver a crushing blow to my hopes…

9 December 2002
Seen in plastic surgery clinic by Mr Q
Saw this lady regarding possible provision of a prosthetic nipple areola complex. We had a superb technician here who made them from impressions of the opposite nipple and the quality of her results far exceeded anything that I could do surgically. Janice obviously heard about this and hence the request to come here. Sadly, the lady in question is on maternity leave and there is some question as to whether or not she will return.

Alas, it had been a wasted journey. My nipple trail had run dry

Foot in Mouth Disease

Some years before, when I reached three years of survival, I had a conversation with one of the dads after Abbie's ballet class.

'My mother had breast cancer,' he said, pleasantly, as if he was telling me that we shared a taste in cars. How sweet, I thought, he's trying to cheer me up. I nodded and smiled. Silence. I helped him along.

'And how is she now?'

He filled me in. 'She's dead,' he said.

I was shocked to the marrow.

'She's dead?'

'Yes.'

'What happened?'

'Oh it came back.'

'When?' I said, not wanting to know.

'Eight years later.'

'Eight years?' I was horrified. 'Eight years later?'

'Yes,' he said.

'But why? Why did it come back?'

'They don't know. You never know. Sometimes it does.'

I wanted to smack him, with his silver-haired good looks and his large house in the country and his very dead mother.

Too late, he realised his mistake.

'But you'll be all right.'

Right…

Living with the Fear

After a while my friends and family stopped worrying that I might die, and I realised that as far as they were concerned, my cancer was over. I was glad for them, and relieved that I could now stop worrying about their worrying. And frankly, I didn't want to think about it either.

The trouble was: I did think about it. Especially when cancer was in the news.

Linda McCartney's death wobbled me. Peggy Butcher's mastectomy wobbled me, even though she was only a fictional character from *Eastenders*. But I said nothing. I didn't want sympathy. I wanted to focus on being well.

So I kept myself busy with constructive, life-enhancing

activities: learning to write better, trying to be a good Mum, obsessing about my breasts: the lack of, size of, shape of, and nipple-less-ness-ness thereof.

I was also busy avoiding breast-cancer awareness month, pink ribbons and fund-raising.

And I was busy coping with the well-meaning friends and the occasional articles they sent about people who'd died from or survived cancer. Smiling though my troubles, I deflected sympathy with a tough outer shell that kept my feelings hidden and my pain safe from prying eyes.

Dr A occasionally trotted me out before his post-grad students as 'the strange case of the woman who refused the adjuvant treatment and lived to tell the tale...' but almost everyone had stopped thinking that my cancer might return.

That is, everyone but me.

And my resolve to hide my feelings so that I might continue to be called 'brave' was beginning to crack.

One evening I went to my spiritual healer training course and we had a session called something like *Death, bereavement and grief: how to deal with it in yourself and others.*

I didn't like this session. Didn't want to do it. Played up, played the fool, played around, disrupted the class, told funnies, bossed everyone in my little group about, didn't let them discuss the issue properly and finally insisted on being the one to give our report to the group so that I could ridicule the whole process.

The tutor, who had every right to be annoyed with me, held my gaze for a long moment and said, 'Why are you so afraid?'

Shocked, I stared back at her, and to my absolute horror, burst into tears.

'Because I don't want to die,' I sobbed. 'I don't want to die.'

Now, that wasn't 'English'. It was embarrassing. Everyone in the room, I decided, was acutely embarrassed. I certainly was.

Afterwards, someone took me aside and whispered that the tutor had been 'out of order'. But I don't think she was out of order. I think she did me a huge favour.

On the way home I started crying again. I wept, wailed, gnashed my teeth, shrieked and would have torn my hair out if only I could have taken my hands off the steering wheel.

I hardly stopped crying for three days. And at the end of it, most of the pain was gone.

I had begun to come to terms with my cancer experience, with losing my breast and living with the fear of dying for all that time without ever telling anyone how I really felt. But expressing my feelings didn't change the fact that I was still afraid. To my mind, every year of survival brought me nearer to the sharp point of that sword of Damocles hanging by a thin horse's hair over my head.

With every year that passed, I felt as if I was getting closer and closer to using up my chances.

When is a Breast not a Breast?

I was sitting quietly on my original plastic surgeon's list as the months and years went by, waiting for the augmentation of my natural breast – my boob job – and for my hernia repair, when someone sent me an article from *The Guardian*.

Clare Rayner had written it in celebration of those women who have the guts – in this breast-obsessed society – to turn down the offer of a reconstruction following mastectomy, and to be content with an empty space and a mastectomy scar.

To illustrate the nobility of this honourable and right-thinking decision, there was a nude photograph of a very beautiful young woman with only one breast. But it wasn't for me. I found it horrific. To me she looked all wrong. Mutilated. Tragic. And by choice.

As it happened, that very day I had an appointment to meet the breast nurse, so I brought the photograph with me.

I bumped into Mr D, my plastic surgeon on the way. I accosted him, as Consultant surgeons don't ordinarily stop to chew the fat with ex-patients in the corridor, and pulled the photograph out of my pocket to show him.

'I just don't understand women who don't have a reconstruction,' I said.

'I couldn't agree more,' he said. 'What's more, I don't understand women who don't go for a reconstructed nipple as well.'

I thought that remark was rather pointed. And it was pointing straight at me. Feeling a little uncomfortable, I said nothing. He pulled out his pen and drew a circle in the margin of the page.

'Look. What do you see?' he said.

'A circle,' I said. He drew a dot in the middle of it.

'Now what do you see?'

'A breast,' I said.

'Exactly,' he said. 'You've just demonstrated your biological programming.'

I realised that he was right. A breast without a nipple is just a mound of flesh.

By a strange coincidence, I was there to investigate the possibility of a reconstructed nipple, though I wasn't going to say that to the man with the knife. The jury was still out on whether I should go for it. But I had been having talks and check-ups with the new breast care nurse. She had invited me to look at her scrapbook and I had come with that purpose in mind.

I found the scrapbook shocking. These were not tasteful photographs of ladies with diaphanous drapes and gently falling sunlight in the back garden of their Surrey homes. It was page after page of post-operative, headless women, with their barely healed mastectomy scars, reconstruction scars and reconstructed nipples.

I was probably one of them, though I was too repulsed to think about that. The scrapbook took me straight back to the early days of the pain and the healing wounds.

I was white and shaking when I came out of there and thanking God that my reconstruction was as good as they had always told me it was, comparatively.

But because of my conversation with the Consultant, I was now hell-bent on getting a reconstructed nipple.

When I had my next appointment with Mr D I told him I was ready. I asked him what he could do for me. He said he could do me a nice augmentation in the right breast to match it with the left one, give me an 'uplift' in both (known as a mastopexy), sort out the little remaining dog ear on my tummy tuck and then reconstruct a nipple when all this had settled down.

It sounded great. I even began to hope that I might end up feeling OK about the way I looked.

29 April 2003
Seen in plastic surgery clinic, by Mr D, Consultant
I reviewed Janice today. Since her weight loss, she has marked asymmetry between her breasts; the right breast being much smaller with some ptosis. Janice would also like to consider nipple reconstruction on the left side and possibly uplifting of the reconstructed breast on the left. I think this is a very reasonable request.

I have gone through the procedure of nipple reconstruction using local skin for the nipple mound and a full thick skin graft from the groin for the areola. I could carry out a mastopexy on the reconstructed breast and slightly uplift the rest of the right breast, placing an implant to get volume match. I have gone over the procedure limitations in great detail with Janice and added her name to my waiting list.

Physician, do thy Worst

It was at this point that I made a terrible mistake. I decided to change my surgeon.

It was nothing that my current surgeon had said or done. It was just that I was in a hurry to be beautiful and his list was long. He said I might have to wait another eighteen months.

And I wanted to get on. I was losing a husband. I needed to look good, to feel good about myself under my clothes. I wanted to have my right breast augmented, both breasts uplifted, and most of all I wanted a nipple.

Why, I thought, I would shortly be a goddess, and irresistible to all mankind.

But this obsession with getting back to normal, an impossible task, was putting strain on my already beleaguered marriage and upsetting my children. Mark was adamantly opposed to the surgery. He said that as far as he was concerned I was a perfectly healthy person who was choosing to mutilate herself. Did I listen? No. I was so afraid, looking like I did, that I was not lovable; that my body made me unlovable; that I would never find another man; and I wanted another man, always, always, always seeking to be loved. And though Mark told me repeatedly that it didn't matter to him what I looked like, I didn't feel loved.

I felt like a freak; a freak who'd begun to picture herself in a world without Mark.

When is a Marriage not a Marriage?

Mark was working as a management Consultant by this time and accepted a contract that took him away from home for three nights a week. I was shocked by my reaction to this, shocked that when he left on Sunday nights my heart rose and when he walked through the door on Wednesdays it sank into my boots. Shouldn't that be the other way around, I thought.

As far as I was concerned, we were pretty much washed up, and I began tentatively to ask for a separation.

It was all very clear to me at the time. He was no good. He wouldn't learn to drive or go into therapy to grapple with his demons and he wouldn't come to counselling with me to try and put it right.

On the other hand, I was no better than he was. I wouldn't keep the house tidy and make his sandwiches and kept asking him piercing questions like, 'Why don't you love me anymore?' to which he answered, 'I do,' which got us nowhere.

But I felt I had evidence that he didn't love me. He didn't want to be with me, talk to me or listen to me.

We argued over the children. He thought that Abbie should be indulged and Michael punished for the tiniest infringements. I, on the other hand, thought that Abbie – who was finally beginning the terrible twos, ten years late – should be disciplined and Michael indulged. Meanwhile, as we quarrelled about the minutest parenting decisions, the children suffered and were damaged.

He thought I was useless and said so. I thought he was a bastard and told him as much.

It wasn't going well.

Mark complained that I was making him jump through hoops for no reason. By this he meant things like asking him to come to counselling or to learn to drive.

The driving thing was a big issue with us.

I made him promise to learn, and he did promise, frequently, just to get his own way over something or to secure a lift somewhere, because promises and sorries tripped lightly off his tongue. But then he wouldn't keep his promises: he wouldn't go for the lessons I had arranged and wouldn't pick up the phone himself to rearrange them. It was maddening.

And all the while, the little voice in my head whispered,

'Stressy Tessy, you need to calm down. Avoid stress, or the cancer will come back and you will die.'

Several times I got so mad with him I threw him out of the car, screaming that if he wouldn't help me to ferry the children around and share the long journeys to see our relatives then he couldn't come in the car with us. But I usually came back for him, repentant and yet seething at my own weakness.

Friends and relatives advised me.

'If he won't learn to drive, just refuse to drive him anywhere.'

But how could I? How could I refuse him, when all the good things about him, the kind and cuddly things, were still there just as they always had been?

It wasn't just about the driving, of course. Relationships are like plants: they grow or they die. They never remain the same. They might look the same on the outside, but inside they're either growing or dying, little by little.

I played my part in our downfall, dancing my half of the Tango backwards and in high heels, as Ginger Rogers put it so eloquently.

I was determined to follow my dream of being a writer and started an MA in screenwriting. I buried myself in my work, going away to writing conferences, neglecting him and the children. When I was around we were either avoiding each other or raging. Only our Sunday evenings, when he cooked and we would cuddle on the sofa and watch TV with the kids, remained an oasis of peace and calm in our increasingly crazy world.

One day I put him out of the car and he had to walk eight

miles home. I didn't go back for him that time; didn't want to. And when he got home he defiantly said that he hadn't needed me to: he'd enjoyed the walk.

Another time when we were in the car he was complaining about something, 'moaning and whingeing' to my mind (for of course I was convinced that my own moaning and whingeing sounded like the soft wind through the poplar trees whilst his sounded like fingernails scraping down a blackboard); and I suddenly became hysterical with rage.

'I've had it with you!' I shouted. 'I've had enough! I told you that your behaviour was destroying our marriage and that one day I wouldn't care anymore and now that day has come.'

I don't know where the words came from but I heard the truth of them at the same time as he did. The day when I no longer cared had come at last.

It was over. I knew I didn't love him. It was gone and would never come back. But he wouldn't leave. He wouldn't even contemplate it. He wouldn't put it right or acknowledge that we even had a problem, but he wouldn't go either. He insisted that he loved me still.

We went to a wedding of one of his work colleagues. The receptionist asked me why they had never seen me at any of the office parties.

'I thought that partners weren't allowed to come,' I said, puzzled.

'Oh,' she said and glanced at Mark curiously. 'But they are. We all bring our partners.'

He had worked there for eight years.

Mark had the grace to look ashamed, while I sat at the

table, humiliated, and in that instant I was certain that I had been right about him not loving me. And not for a long time either.

It was very sad. And no wonder I had lost the plot with my body image, when once upon a time the plot, which had included Mark, had seemed so clear.

It was difficult to decide what to do about my breasts, and in the end I decided to go forward and have the operation, since I couldn't go backward and become what I once was. No one can. And standing still – being happy with what I was – I just couldn't do that yet, no matter how much I knew inside that I was being ridiculous. The problem, the real problem didn't come from my belief that I had lost my looks as a result of the operation. It came from not believing that I was beautiful in the first place.

1963 Am I Pretty, Mummy?

I had a feeling that I might be. Ever since I could focus I had been looking at pictures of princesses and fairies, and was satisfied that I was not dissimilar: I had two eyes, a nose and a mouth, just like them. As for the rest, Mummy would know. She knew everything.

But first it occurred to me that my hairstyle could do with some adjustment. I was well qualified to do that, since I knew how to hold a pair of scissors, and saw no need whatsoever to involve anyone else. So one fine autumn day the afternoon sun found me hiding under the kitchen table with the largest pair of scissors in the house.

The matter of hiding was merely pragmatic, of course; not an admission of guilt, but a small precaution against the interference of itinerant snoopers.

It wasn't long before I had systematically cut all my abundant, curly, copper-coloured hair into interesting little tufts. Ten years later, in the punk age, I would have been a huge success. But even in 1963, I thought I looked just fine.

When the furore had died down and my hair had been cut properly at the hairdresser's, I asked my Mum – the fount of all wisdom – for a final verdict on the question of my good looks.

She was washing up and I tugged at her apron. Mums in those days always wore aprons. They were real Mums. They wore aprons and on Sunday afternoons, after cooking a roast dinner, they ironed socks and folded handkerchiefs.

I looked up at her, turning my face towards her like a flower stretching up to the sun. This was the judge's sentence and would form the blueprint for my physical esteem for ever and ever.

'Am I pretty, Mummy?'

I waited while she screwed up her face so hard that she was almost gurning – almost but not quite – since even my talented Mum could not gurn successfully with her teeth in.

The screwed up face spelled indecision to me and fear trembled softly in my stomach.

Mum struggled to answer. She wobbled desperately between her need to grow a child that wasn't a 'show-off' and her talent for gardening, knowing as any good gardener knows that *plants and children need roots, the strong firm roots of self-esteem. And sadly for me she jumped the wrong way.*

That fateful day she denied her horticultural talent and her desire to grow beautiful, strong, enduring children and she blundered through my fragile roots with her best pruning shears.

'Not pretty,' she said, putting the sixth dinner plate in the drying rack. 'Bonny, maybe.'

'What's that?' I said, stricken with disappointment, my shoulders feeling suddenly burdensome. Not a princess then? Not for me, the handsome prince and castle?

'Not quite pretty.' She shook her head. 'Just bonny. That'll do. You'll get by with that.'

Ingredients: 1 Bra, 1 Bag of Rice, 1 Set of Scales, 1 Brain

Mr P, my new plastic surgeon after I'd unceremoniously dumped Mr D on account of my impatience to attain physical perfection, was breathtakingly handsome. What's more he had the whitest shirt I'd ever seen since I last saw a policeman.

I found his looks and his laundry so encouraging that I instantly gave up on the idea of seeing examples of his work and decided there and then to go with him. The truth is: I had a momentary loss of brain function.

Now, I'm not casting nasturtiums on Mr P's surgical prowess. In fact, I would never do that, because I believe nasturtiums are a plant and that I'm thinking of... some other word.

Anyway, at the first appointment, Mr P and his lovely assistant pointed out that I was lacking a groove between my breasts, which, I think, not all women have. Certainly I had never had one.

But Mr P said that a proper cleavage between the breasts is more attractive.

I said I'd better have one then.

Then he said that I also needed an inframammary fold.

'Good God,' I said. 'What's that?'

Mr P explained that ideally I should be able to hold a pencil in place under my breasts, which I couldn't do.

I agreed that I was clearly lacking in that department, so I'd better have one of those while they were about it.

Turning his attention finally to the original matter of the implant, Mr P told me to go home, fill a plastic bag with rice and stick it in the left-hand side of my bra, then weigh the bag of rice and let him know the outcome. I wondered if I had heard him correctly. He explained: the bag of rice would play the role of the implant by filling out the bra. Then if I weighed it and reported the weight to him, he would know how big an implant to put in.

I was highly impressed by this, so did as I was told and came up with the figure of 230 grams. Though nobody told me at the time, this was quite a bit bigger than the 150ml implant they'd originally envisaged.

So the plan was for me to have the implant, the groove between the breasts and the fold under the breasts all in one go. Then, when that had settled down, the surgeon would make me a reconstructed nipple.

Time passed and eventually I went into hospital for the operation, alone. Mark had already made his feelings about unnecessary surgery clear and would have nothing to do with any of it.

All the other couples had partners with them and I felt Mark's absence keenly.

That notwithstanding, I was thrilled to bits at the prospect of having similar-sized breasts again, plus a new place to keep my pencils and a cleavage my visitors could park their bikes in.

And so I went under the knife yet again, with hope singing in my heart. When I came to I inspected my bandaged breast. From what I could see, which wasn't that much, it looked fine. The fold under the left breast was a definite improvement, although the cleavage didn't seem to be happening. I didn't mind that; it hadn't mattered to me before and didn't matter to me now.

I was happy with my new breast. At first.

2 July 2004
Seen in breast clinic by Mr C

I was pleased to review Janice today. As you know, she has recently undergone mastopexy of her right breast with revision of her previous left breast reconstruction and abdominal scar. She is very pleased with the result and indeed it looks a very good result all round. I gather there is going to be some delay before consideration of reconstruction of the left nipple.

She is still aware of slight fullness in the lower right abdomen. I was unconvinced there was a hernia. I have fully reassured her. We will review her in 6 months. Once the recent revision of the right breast has settled, it would be appropriate to follow her up with further ultrasound scan.

It's true. I did report to the oncologist Mr C that I was very happy with the breast reconstruction, but I spoke too soon. That was before the bandages came off.

When they did, I discovered that the handsome surgeon had put the implant in by cutting around my existing aureole and lifting out my nipple, instead of the usual way, which is underneath the breast, where the scars are not visible. So I was left with a nipple that was pulled out of shape and a breast that was now much larger than the reconstructed one.

To recap:

I started off with two natural breasts, of near-perfect symmetry.

Then I got cancer and had a simultaneous mastectomy and reconstruction, after which the natural breast – the right one – and the reconstructed breast – the left one – were still roughly the same size.

Then I lost four and a half stone in weight, so the right breast shrank considerably and ended up two sizes smaller than the left, reconstructed, breast.

Then, to even them up again, I had an implant placed in the right breast by a surgeon I'd chosen on account of his good looks, and who had asked me to put a bag of rice in my bra. However, this was too big and the right breast was now at least one size larger than the other one, and the only nipple I had left was a peculiar shape.

Oh dear. Why hadn't I just left it alone?

I decided to conduct a thorough investigation into what had

gone wrong. The surgeon said he had inserted an implant of 285ml. Even with my little brain I thought I could see a big difference between the figure of 230g (which I had given him) and 285ml (which he had given me).

But it turned out I was muddling up my maths as usual. I consulted a professorial friend of mine on the mystery of my enormous breast implant, and he tried to explain.

Subject: Gs vs Mls

Hi Janice,

Did the experiment; results are quite interesting. As I told you on the phone, rice is denser than water and thus sinks when added. However, this is more than compensated for by air gaps between grains, so that a pile of rice occupies more volume than a 'pile' of water of the same weight.

Experiment using basmati rice:-

800mls of water weighs 800g by definition (at 4 degrees C strictly speaking)

800mls volume of rice found to weigh 640g.

Therefore, 1g rice occupies 800/640 = 1.25mls volume

Therefore, 230g weight of rice occupies 230x1.25= 287.5mls volume.

Regrettably, the surgeon was correct within a whisker.

All the best, Prof TW

I will just have to take his word for it on that one, since this analysis is completely beyond the understanding of someone who has only just got the hang of decimalisation, let alone the metric system. But it looks like the mismatch of size between the two breasts was down to my miscalculation, and perhaps the fact that I was wearing a push-up bra and the bag of rice pushed my breast out of it, like a cuckoo… or something.

Suffice to say that I ended up after the operation with two differently sized tits, which was unfortunate, because that's where I started.

So what did I do?

I went back to have the left breast made bigger. Despite my now oddly shaped natural nipple, I actually liked the implant in the right. It reminded me of my old friend the outplant, only covered in skin. It was nice to play with too, like a built-in executive toy.

14 October 2004
Seen in plastic surgery clinic by Mr P, Consultant
I have reviewed this lady in outpatients following revision of left breast reconstruction and mastopexy with implant on the right breast. The wounds are now fully healed and the new inframammary fold created for the left breast seems stable.

There is at present a slight volume and shape difference between the breasts and as the left breast base is considerably wider than the right, we have discussed the possibility of a symmetrising procedure involving liposuction to the medial and lateral aspects of the left breast and fat transfer to the central mound of the same side.

I have booked her in for surgery on the 7th January 2005 and will keep you informed of her progress.

Time for a Think

I had a think after that appointment. Finally, I had a think.

Mr P was now saying that he wanted me to have an extra operation before the left breast implant. And the reason seemed to be that he didn't like the shape of my left breast.

Then, when my body had recovered from the reshaping and resizing of its left breast, he would make me a nipple, probably using a skin graft from the other nipple – the real one – which was, of course, a more appealing idea than scavenging my private parts.

I decided that in his enthusiasm he was getting a little carried away. Whose body was this anyway? Or, to be specific, whose body image was in charge here? My image of my body? Or his image of my body?

I hadn't come to have operations so that I could hold pencils under my breasts, park bikes between them and change their shape when I had no problem with their shape.

I just wanted breasts the same size, and two nipples. I knew other women had different sized breasts. But mine had been symmetrical before the cancer got hold of me, and in truth that was at the heart of my problem. I wanted so much to go back to where I was before it all began. Was that too much to ask, I whined, internally. Of course it was, but I wanted it anyway.

I got in such a muddle I hardly knew what I thought about it at all, until the day of the operation dawned and everything suddenly became clear.

When they came to take me down to surgery to change the shape of my reconstructed breast, which I had always thought was perfectly all right, I told them that I didn't want that. I just wanted to go straight to the finishing post and have an implant so that the two breasts matched in size, which, I pointed out politely, was why I had come to them in the first place.

The anaesthetist scratched his chin and called the Registrar. The Registrar hemmed and hawed and called the Consultant. And after a short kerfuffle, I bent them to my will.

There is nothing like being chopped about willy-nilly by surgeons to teach you basic assertiveness.

In standing up for my left breast, the one that the original surgeon had fashioned so lovingly all those years ago, I had an epiphany.

It didn't matter what I looked like. It only mattered what I *thought* I looked like. And all the surgery in the world wouldn't change that.

That sounded very sensible. The trouble was, I *thought* I look like a pig's ear. And if I looked like a pig's ear without my clothes, who was ever going to love me again?

Time to Move On

Even though I was terrified of being alone, I knew that time was up for Mark and me. And by 2005, I had been quietly working on him for a few years. Well, when I say quietly, it was more like frequent requests for him to leave, expressed in subtle terms such as:

'When are you moving out?'

Subtlety was never my forte. But one time I caught him in the right mood and said the right thing.

He had returned from work to the ever-present domestic

and emotional chaos and complained bitterly as usual. He was hurtful in these latter years, saying that he was fed up with the messy, cluttered house, reiterating again and again that I was useless, and once even telling me how much I was polluting the atmosphere just by being in it.

I reacted calmly for a change, pointing out that I don't pollute 'the' atmosphere, just his.

'Imagine what it would be like if you didn't have to experience this?' I said, gently. 'What if you could come home to your own cool flat, quiet and empty and all yours, with no noise and clutter? Why are you resisting this separation when you know it's what you want?' He looked up at me and I could see my words sink in.

A week or so after that, he came home with a stripe down the middle of his face – a graze, in fact – and said that he'd just had a spiritual experience and was ready to move out. Surprised, I asked him to explain.

Walking along that morning, he had passed some discarded cardboard boxes beside a skip and caught his foot in a loop of the tough plastic twine they use to tie them. He'd gone down like a sack of potatoes and hit his face. Bam. This told him, he said, that he had been refusing to see something that was staring him right in the face, until it hit him, right in the face.

'What was it?' I said, knowing the answer.

'That we are not going to grow old together. That we need to move on.'

I had mixed emotions then. I couldn't tell him he was wrong because I knew he was right. I knew that we needed to get out of this trap of bitter arguments and hurtful words because we were damaging each other and the children. Couples may have 'put up with it' in the olden days, but they were wrong.

So whilst I was exhilarated beyond description, I was terribly sad and afraid too.

But of course, Mark, being Mark, did nothing about it. And because I was afraid of being a single parent – and for my children – I did nothing about it either.

Until I had a spiritual experience of my own.

Through the Looking-Glass

It happened like this. I was in Athens, on a writing course. One morning, in a lecture on neuro-linguistic-programming, I suddenly gasped out loud. I had just realised that I had left my purse in the bedside table drawer of the room I had been moved from, on account of the fact that it had flooded.

The lecturer said 'What's the matter with you?' The word 'now' hung silently in the air for all to imagine, for she knew me well.

Because she was Greek, I adopted the language of a nineteenth-century romantic novelist in my reply. As everybody knows, when talking to a foreign person one must either shout as if they are extremely deaf, or slip into Jane Austen-speak. It's the only way.

I did the latter and said, 'There is a matter to which I must attend.'

'Go on then,' she said, her English being a lot better than mine, so I ran out of the room. That was meant to demonstrate to everyone that I wasn't really the old crock that I appeared to be. Of course, it had the opposite effect, since I was not running, but lolloping.

I had been sitting at the front, so I lolloped down the side of the lecture room and veered left through the sliding glass door.

I need to watch where I put my feet because I am always spraining my ankles. But on this occasion I was concentrating so hard on them that I didn't pay any attention to what my head was doing, which was hitting the sliding glass doors. I hadn't noticed that they were closed, despite the fact that they were tinted and bore a huge logo at head height.

The glass didn't like it. It cracked all the way down, and smashed into smithereens.

I suddenly found myself flying through the air in slow motion just as people do in books and films, with fragments of glass falling around me like beautiful snowflakes. There was at least one huge section of glass falling vertically towards me, like that bit in *The Omen* where his head gets chopped off.

While this was going on there was the most beautiful sound of breaking glass – the biggest sound of breaking glass you ever heard, big enough to satisfy a packed Wembley Stadium – and it filled the room around and above and behind me and rang out like a clarion call to the other delegates that something was amiss.

Wonderful, it was.

And still I flew: slowly, slowly, and with my foot tripping over the metal runner of the sliding door I flew on through the air and after what seemed like an eon of time I came to rest with a terrific scrunch in the glass that now completely covered the carpet beneath.

Then there were people all around me, helping me up, and there was blood trickling down my face, and me saying 'Have I broken my nose?' as if anyone could really tell, and someone saying 'Where were you running off to in such a hurry?': a question I couldn't possibly answer, since I couldn't even remember who I was, let alone where I was going.

Later, everyone said I should be dead, or maimed, or bleeding to death. But I wasn't. The Greek chambermaids kept coming up to me and patting me on the head, smiling and nodding, as if my survival was miraculous, which it was.

I ran through a plate glass door and walked away with only a tiny, tiny scar on my nose and two more tiny ones on my hand and some fabulously spectacular bruises that I dined out on for weeks afterwards. Of course I felt like a complete arse, but what was new about that?

Like all major experiences, this one spoke to me. It said I should go forward in life, no matter where; that whatever I do, no matter how terrifying and painful it might seem, if I proceed with determination and strength of purpose I will crash through the pain barrier and be supported by the universe and I will be safe. It was a kind of affirmation of the 'Feel the fear and do it anyway' school of thought.

So I went home and asked Mark to leave. Straightaway.

And within a few weeks, he was gone.

1987 Nuclear-Infested Family

My Dad was special. He was part of the team that designed the machine that split the atom – or he single-handedly invented it, depending on how inventive I am feeling myself when I tell this story.

He also went to the Christmas Islands in the late Fifties to test atom bombs, just before impregnating my mother with his 'nuclear-infested' sperm, which she of course insists is why I got cancer.

Thirty years after the testing of the atom bomb and just before he shuffled off his mortal coil, Dad told my sister Jane that he was worried because people from that original team were dying of cancer. I was excited when she told me this. I heard faint echoes of the curse of Tutankhamen's tomb. But then, I'm as mad as my Mum.

Alas, we were never able to prove the theory that his card was marked, because he shuffled off his mortal coil and dropped dead of a heart attack before the evil prophecy could play itself out. It turns out now that he may have been right, but at the time we gave our own diagnosis: Dad smoked, drank and lived on bubble-and-squeak and sausages, until one day his heart blew up.

He was *fifty-seven years old. According to Jane, he hadn't visited the doctor for fourteen years. He had been to Sunday lunch with her one day and complained of pains in his chest, which he insisted were caused by indigestion. A few days later he called the surgery and said his indigestion was very bad. The doctor said he would come at once. He told Dad to go and lie down, but when he arrived at the flat no one answered the door. Fearing the worst, the doctor fetched the police to break it down and they found Dad inside. He wasn't being anti-social. He was just dead.*

While he was lying on his bed, alone in his death throes, I was on a boat with university friends, coming back to Oban from the Island of Lismore in western Scotland.

Try as I might to remember some stillness, some fey sense of my father's passing, I cannot. Whilst I looked at the gently rolling sea and wept at leaving Scotland, my father breathed his last breath alone.

As there were no traces of my Mum in his flat, they couldn't track her down for a couple of days. I was back in London when she rang to let me know.

'It's your Dad,' she said. 'Your Dad's dead.'

'No...'

That first cry, wrenched from me by my mother's words, was my way of saying that we had unfinished business, my Dad and I. There hadn't been enough years, enough real conversations like the one we had had a few months before, when he told me a version of my childhood that I longed to believe, in which he was the hero, misunderstood and pilloried by all.

And then there was the matter of his old age, when I might have tended him, lost to me now; and now my Dad's arms never to be around me, and me never to sit on his knee again – which I probably wouldn't have – but nevertheless, I felt that he was snatched untimely from his daughter's arms.

I caught the train to my mother's house and slept on her sofa.

The next day we went to the police station in Reading. I had to sign for his things because I was his next of kin. The others weren't his relatives; they were my half-siblings, the progeny of my mother's first marriage.

It was weird that I, the youngest, the one who had never had any power in the family beyond the power to make mischief, had suddenly become central. I was my father's daughter. In law, he had no wife and no other children. There was only me.

The policeman handed me a fan.

'What's this?' I said.

'That's all the money he had on him,' said the policeman behind the counter. I looked closely at the fan. It was made of pound notes, spread out and pinned together.

'But why do you do this?' I said, holding it very carefully. I was offended, but also awed: they had made my Dad into a beautiful tidy clean thing, a fan, lovingly fashioned by strangers in bright crisp uniforms. What was the meaning of that, I wondered.

'We just do. That's what we do.' He was flustered. I don't think anyone had ever complained before. I reassured him.

'It's so pretty,' I said. 'Isn't it pretty, Mum?' I showed it to her and she nodded at me and smiled a little. She and the policeman exchanged glances.

'Come on,' she said, and I signed my name to receive his clothes and his keys and his pretty fan of thirty quid: all he had on him, as the policeman said.

My brother John had driven us over to Reading and he took us to the hospital to see the body, though he didn't want to come in. It was unpleasant but important. It told me that he was dead.

My Dad was all dolled up with mascara and lipstick. He had bright pink cheeks and Grecian 2000 on his hair. One eye squinted open slightly, the way a cat's does when it's asleep and has forgotten to shut its outer lid.

The creature on the table wasn't my Dad. But despite the monkey they had made out of him, it was quite obviously my Dad's body.

So if that was his body and he wasn't in it, he must definitely be gone and I would have to accept the fact. Seeing the empty body helped me through the grieving process. As the Americans are fond of saying, it provided closure.

We went back to the car and John drove us to Dad's flat, which Mum had never seen. I stood in the poky little corridor, not knowing which room to go into, since they were all empty of my Dad. My brother came out of the bedroom. He had discovered Dad's HND certificate for Electronics Engineering. He held it and wept.

He told me that he hadn't spoken to Dad for ten years. He had written him a letter – one of those deep dark letters that people sometimes write to their parents – to which Dad had never replied.

We stood awkwardly together in the corridor, sharing that

moment of my brother's grief for the man he hated.

My mother appeared beside us, calm, as if she had discovered some deep truth. We looked at her, waiting for her contribution to this fragile moment.

'He left the immersion heater on,' she said, tossing her head in disgust. 'Typical!'

Screwing Up the Kids

Mark and I were so caught up in our drama that we didn't notice that we had planned for him to move out two days before Abbie's twelfth birthday, a blunder for which she may never forgive us. Thirteen-year-old Michael was upset too, telling us in studiedly casual tones that we should get our act together and not split up at all, before turning back to his Xbox.

Overwhelmed with guilt, and so desperate to give the children a different experience of their parents' divorce than I had of mine, I devised a cunning plan; one of my brilliant ideas that actually made the whole thing ten times worse for everyone.

I proclaimed that even though Mum and Dad were going to stop living in the same building at the same time, the children would stay put. Nothing would actually change as far as the children were concerned, I said. We would always be a family.

Sweeping Mark along with me in my enthusiasm, I persuaded him that the children should not be made to suffer just because we couldn't live together. 'Why should they be shunted about?' I said. I determined that we were the ones that should be shunted.

He agreed, seeing some merit in the idea, so we rented a flat not far away and took it in turns to live there ourselves, leaving the children 'stable' at home. We set the changeover every four nights so that it rolled around the calendar in a blur of dates, although I marked it up with pink and blue dots so that the children could see at a glance which one of us was supposed to be parent-in-residence, if they felt the need to know.

I thought it would be like that children's game of drawing in the corner of each page of a notebook and then flicking through it so fast that the drawings become animated cartoons. There would be parents coming and going so fast that the children wouldn't even notice that they only had one parent at a time.

The doctor was impressed. The teachers were impressed. Everyone thought it was innovative and inspired.

It wasn't. It was absolutely crazy.

Mark and I coped so badly with shunting ourselves about that we nearly went round the bend. I took more and more of my belongings every time, dragging bigger and bigger suitcases up the road with me. And we both competed to leave the flat or the house in perfect condition so that neither of us could hurl accusations of slovenliness at the other, which made 'changeover' day a nightmare of obsessive cleaning and clockwatching. Then at five o'clock precisely, one parent would drag their case up the path while the other stomped down it.

And I was still their Mum, still taking most of the responsibility for them. When it was Mark's turn to be parent-in-residence he continued to travel into London every day, stubbornly refusing to contemplate working from home. And because I didn't want the children to be latch-key kids – I remembered too well how bleak that felt – I still went back to the house in time to greet Michael with his tea after school and then dashed back to the flat in time to greet Abbie with hers. The flat was positioned between her school and the house and she liked to drop in there and wait until Daddy arrived home from London and could pick her up on his way home.

Guilt-ridden, I was bending over backwards to please everyone with this scheme and failing utterly. Instead of celebrating the return of one parent every four days, the children were far more aware of being abandoned by other. It was a disaster.

Our break-up affected them badly. Michael refused to do any work at school and stared out of the window all day. Abbie, on the other hand, who had always been perfectly behaved until our marriage started to slip down the pan, stopped going to school altogether, and nothing I did would persuade her, so that she ended up eventually being educated online at home.

One day, after six months of this torment, I arrived home to take up the mantle of parent-in-residence and found Mark staring vacantly at his suitcase. I flopped into a chair, feeling as exhausted and desperate as he looked. He turned a haggard face to me and said, 'I can't go on like this.'

I was surprised, but after a moment's thought I saw that he was right.

'Ok,' I said. 'Let's stop. You stay in the flat and I'll stay in the house.' Everyone, even the building itself, seemed to breathe a huge sigh of relief.

The cunning plan had failed. And I realised at once that it

was all born out of guilt; out of my desperate desire to avoid the accusation that I had committed the same sin as my mother.

I had deprived the children of their Dad.

1969 Leaving Dad

In the months before my parents' separation a grey cloud of misery hung over our home. It left the house with me in the morning, waited for me at the school gates and greeted me when I came out.

I knew, young as I was, that I would at some point be called upon to take sides, so I decided not to wait for the axe to fall and took my mother's. I stopped seeking out my father's company and muttered sullen answers to his attempts to bridge the gap.

I tried to talk about the impending split at school, but was hushed. Divorce was outside my friends' experience, a social gaffe like early menstruation (a sin I had already committed), or going down with The Big C (the sin of my future).

The day came, at last, when my mother took me aside to tell me what was happening. Her mouth was a grim cartoon line, savagely dividing her upper face from her chin.

The mouth moved. 'Your father and I are getting a divorce,' it said. 'The others are coming with me. What do you want to do?'

'I'll come with you.'

I had already made my decision, painstakingly cutting my father out of my heart with a pair of child's safety scissors. He was already dead to me.

I told my school friends that it was actually happening, no longer an idle, sensationalist threat but my reality. I heard the whispers, almost out of earshot, and for a little while the cool anaesthetic cream of celebrity slid sweetly over my wounds and it felt good.

On the day my family left my Dad, my once-darling Dad, and while my childhood was packed up into cardboard boxes and carried out to the van, I went to say goodbye to the field at the top of the road.

I climbed up onto the six-foot gate and gazed around me for the last time. Somehow I knew I would never see the place again. I mentally photographed the line of trees that hid the spring garden and the beloved field of my youth, committing to memory the copse on the far left where we built our dens, the wild sweep of grasses, spattered with buttercups and daisies, where one summer we threw ourselves again and again, desperately inhaling the pollen in the hope that we might catch hay fever and 'get off school' like Andy Jones.

There was the log where we played kissing games with some greater-spotted youths and whispered to each other that one day we might do 'It'. But not with Simon Banks, definitely not with him. There on the far right, beneath the trees, was the place where the stream that ran across the field went to ground. We spent hours damming that stream, clogging it up with twigs and stones and great mounds of earth so that it flooded the neighbouring gardens and brought the wrath of the grown-ups down on us.

There was the murky bog where I lost my Wellington boots and had to go home without them in the rain.

There, especially, was the hollow tree, where one day Patsy Parkin and I had found the gnome.

I heard my mother calling me to get into the removal van.

They were ready to go. Still perched up on the gate, I undid the latch and pushed off from the past with one small sandalled foot, savouring the very last swing I would ever have on that big gate.

The van was waiting with its engine running. There was no sign of Dad.

I didn't go into the house to find him and I didn't look back. He didn't try to visit us and I didn't see him again for a long time.

Many years later I asked him why he hadn't come out to say goodbye.

'Why didn't you come in?' he said. 'You didn't say goodbye to me either.'

I didn't answer. I was in my twenties then, struggling with my damage in secret. It was before therapy and psycho-babble rescued me from ignorance and confusion. But even then some part of me knew that he was wrong; some part of me knew that grown-ups are supposed to be braver and less needy than their children.

I didn't bother to say so. It seemed to me that if he hadn't known it when I was a child what was the point of telling him when I was an adult?

It was too late.

Getting Things Sorted

After the second implant – the one to my left breast – when I had asserted my right not to be fiddled with willy-nilly, I walked out of that hospital and vowed never to come back.

Well, only for check-ups, then.

I decided to pursue my original idea of a stick-on nipple and found a master craftsman for the job. Of course, it had to be distorted and peculiar-looking to match the one on the right. It took some weeks to make, but it turned out well.

When I went back to see the beautiful plastic surgeon for a check-up, I wore my new accessory and he had difficulty remembering 'which boobie was the poorly one' (as five-year-old Michael had so aptly put it all those years ago).

I couldn't imagine a better testimony to the expertise of the nipple-maker than that.

28 July 2005
Seen in plastic surgery clinic, by Mr P
Janice has had numerous operations to reconstruct the breast. Her last operation in January involved a breast implant and liposuction to axillary tail of the upper quadrant on the left side.

She was due to have a nipple reconstructed but has since had a prosthetic nipple made at Roehampton. On examination today the prosthetic nipple–areola complex is an excellent cosmetic match to the other side and Janice is very happy with the outcome. She is not keen for any further surgery at the moment but is happy for us to keep her under review, and I am therefore going to see Janice again routinely in 1 year's time at her request.

Recall due: 04/02/2007

The Brilliant Career

For all the pain and angst of the break-up, the damage to the kids, the financial difficulties and the burden of bringing up two teenagers on my own, I don't regret splitting up with Mark. The bitter rows have gone. My home is a haven of peace and tranquillity. My children and I enjoy each other and are loving (as long as I do as I'm told and give them money). I'm so proud of them sometimes I almost burst with love. Don't tell them. They are teenagers and might throw up.

Even Mark and I are civil to each other now and may yet be friends, all being well.

It was time to begin my new life, beginning with my career.

There were only two things I was ever really any good at. One was singing and the other was writing.

It seemed to me that in choosing to be a singer I had jumped the wrong way. I did it for the wrong reasons, looking for love, always looking to be loved. I never really wanted to be a performer for a living and the struggle had made me unhappy.

Being a wannabe is bad enough, but being a reluctant wannabe is like trying to walk the catwalk in shoes that are two sizes too small. Not only is it difficult, it's also extremely painful.

As for writing?

Once, Peter Cook was introduced to a stranger at a party in the following way. The hostess said, 'This is John and he's writing a novel.' Peter smiled and nodded wisely at the man.

'Neither am I, darling,' he said. 'Neither am I.'

He expressed so eloquently the syndrome from which

wannabe writers suffer. We pretend we are afraid of success because it sounds so grand, but actually we are afraid of failure; hence we practise not-writing.

I had spent many years not-writing that novel. I had also not-written an autobiography, not-written an autobiographical novel and finally not-written a memoir.

Not-writing is extremely time-consuming, as anyone who practises it will tell you.

It was time for me to stop not-writing and finish my book.

You Show Me Yours and I'll Show You Mine

Was it also time to stop my sad search for the body beautiful?

It is my firm opinion that cosmetic surgery will first become commonplace...

...and then become addictive...

...and then will carry a government health warning...

...and then will come with patches to help us all give up, which will probably take the form of large hoods with eye-holes...

...and will finally become illegal...

...and go underground...

...and fall into the hands of charlatans...

...and then we will all be walking around looking like the Phantom of the Opera.

I googled *Dr Susan Love's Breast Book* to see if her wonderful book had survived and found its way onto the internet.

It had. I found a website bursting with helpful information about breast cancer and sporting photographs of half-naked women, who had all had reconstructive breast surgery.

It was strange. Like everybody else I'm used to seeing the breasts of glamour models and film stars, but most women don't look like that.

The reality is that my breasts look not dissimilar to the next person's. Not completely the same, but not completely different either.

The other thing that struck me about these photographs was that all the women were smiling. There they were, thrusting out their peculiar, dangling, malformed chests and smiling with happiness. They were not pretending to smile. They really were smiling. Why? I sought answers to these questions and found them with a friend.

She had followed a similar path to mine in her quest for symmetry and a stick-on nipple.

I said I'd show her mine if she showed me hers. She responded with good humour and got them out.

There they were. Large, strangely shaped things that men would recognise easily as breasts. But what did I see?

I saw a beautiful woman.

When I was a teenager and had a zit the night of an important date, I thought it was huge and pulsating and neon. And that's what it had been like for me those ten long years. Under my clothes I felt like a walking mass of scars, like a large roly-poly map of the London Underground. And I thought of myself as the sum total of all my scars.

Yes, my friend had scars, too. She also had some inequality of breast shape and size and volume and a stuck-on nipple that was so lifelike it was scary and at the same time wasn't quite real.

But despite and beyond and through all that, I saw *her*, with her lovely face and womanly shape and all her experiences of life and her hopes for the future. And I thought she looked beautiful.

I didn't get it before. I never got it.

The reality – the harsh reality – is that I had operations that I didn't need because I wanted to look... how?

Similar to... better than... more than... less than... just anything but... *me*.

Was I finally ready to stand still and be myself?

On the Subject of S. E. X.

It was difficult to contemplate dating when I knew that sooner or later the question of how many nipples I had was going to come up.

Before I ventured forth into the world, I was fascinated to hear about the experiences of a girlfriend who had already had a reconstruction and whose marriage was stone cold in its grave. She told me she had started internet dating. I was shocked. I knew she had a stick-on nipple for one thing. What about that?

There was another issue: her cancer had spread. She was living on borrowed time against a ticking clock and one tiny step ahead of the Grim Reaper. She knew her number was up; it was all crumbling into bollockdom and she was completely buggered.

I asked her if the man she was meeting knew about her

cancer. She demurred, saying there was a time for that and this wasn't it. I thought she should have told him. Damaged goods and all that. But then, I realised, the question of disclosure isn't so easy. At what point could she have brought it up? In the advertisement? Something along the lines of: 'Sexy soon-to-be-dead cancer victim seeks romp with freak-lover. All prosthetic appliances welcome.'

But it was hard. How many fifty-year-old women have any confidence in their normal fifty-year-old bodies to cope with dating, let alone slightly wacky, slightly off-the-wall, slightly horribly-mutilated bodies?

The men who are 'doing you a favour' don't help either, though they are obviously trying. My first foray into sex-after-marriage happened to be with a man who actively sought out unusual body types. Humps, wooden legs, bearded ladies. He just loved 'em.

When I found this out afterwards it knocked my confidence somewhat. Just a little.

But before I put my toe in the water, I pumped my friend for information. I asked her if the stick-on nipple had been a success. She said, 'Not really. It doesn't feel too good. Also, I've found, their hands can actually get stuck on it and pull it off, which is not ideal either.'

'What do you do then?'

'Just gently guide their hands away.

'Don't they notice?' I asked.

'No,' she said. 'I dated one guy I'd slept with years before and I honestly don't think he noticed that I'd had a mastectomy at all.'

'Was he partially sighted?'

'No!' she said, sharply.

The don't-mention-it-and-you-can-be-sure-they-won't-notice way was her way, but it wouldn't work for me, even though I remember being horribly put off once by a man who arrested my hand as it crept into his trousers to tell me that he only had one bollock. Would I have noticed, I wonder?

No, despite my own experiences of being put off by honest disclosure, I found myself compelled to stand naked in front of my suitors and give them a thorough and detailed tour around my scars.

That's my style.

And if they still had an erection, we were on.

But it felt like a trial by drowning, like witch-trials where if the plaintiff were innocent of witchery she would not float, so she drowned; and if she turned out to be a witch and floated, she was torched.

If my suitors still had an erection by the end of the tour, I knew they were either insensitive, incorrigible sex addicts, or fully paid-up members of the freak-show club. And if they hadn't got an erection – if they'd either left by the nearest exit, or were holding me in their arms while we both sobbed quietly into each other's chest hair – then… well… that was a bit of a dampener too.

But the good news is that on the whole men are simpler creatures than us and – in the area of sex – also better creatures.

Let's face it, they're desperate, most of them, and being desperate, they really aren't that choosy. At least, that's what I found. So after the sobbing, the erections came back.

And I guess that's what I'm trying to say. After the sobbing, the erections come back.

Laying the Ghosts to Rest

Even though it was nine years since the cancer had started, I still remembered the silver-haired man's story about his mother's cancer returning eight years later.

Finally, I determined to ask Mr C the question I had buried for so long.

I told him that I had begun dreading my annual visits with him.

'Why?' he said, curiously.

'Because I have this idea in my head that I have used up all my chances now,' I said, 'as if I have been playing Russian Roulette with the same gun and firing one shot a year. And with each year that passes it is becoming more and more likely that the cancer will return.'

He smiled at me. 'Quite the opposite,' he said. 'In fact, with each year that passes, it is becoming less and less likely that the cancer will return.'

I stared at him. Could that really be true?

'Honestly?'

'Yes. In fact, most women with a 50:50 chance of surviving ten years die in the first five.'

Suddenly I was cross. All those long years, thinking I was getting closer and closer to death.

'Why didn't you tell me that in the first place?'

'Because it would have worried you,' he said.

He was right. Of course it would.

4 February 2005
Seen in breast clinic, by Mr C, Consultant

Further to previous correspondence, I saw Janice again today. She seems very well. She has obviously had a very good result following her revisional breast surgery. As you know, she now has an implant in both breasts. She is pleased with the outcome.

From the hernia point of view, there is still I think a weakness in the lower right side of her abdominal wall. This however does not amount to a hernia and I think merely reflects the presence of the mesh overlying generally weak oblique muscle.

There is certainly nothing to suggest recurrence of her breast cancer. It is now 9 years since her original treatment. I think on that basis it would be reasonable to discontinue routine follow-up. She is happy with this arrangement. Obviously if you or she has any concerns I would be happy to see her sooner.

She will be 50 in a couple of years' time.

Finding Myself

The other day I went to visit the house of my childhood. First I drove to the top of the road and tried to see any trace of our old haunts. But my premonition that the field would no longer be there had been right. The road didn't end in the big six-foot gate as it used to. That had disappeared. Instead, it carried straight through onto an ugly housing estate.

Not long after we left my father, the Council bought the big private estate we children had thought of as our own and built a huge development over it, leaving only the little spring garden, enclosed as it always was by its own ancient red brick wall.

Like many of the elderly, it sat there, bewildered, and exuded disdain amongst the council houses that curled around it in neat ugly rows. Perhaps it was remembering more elegant times, laughing children; beautiful adults. Perhaps it was just a garden.

And what had happened to the laughing children I played with there?

Kathy Carter went to work for the Council and ended up as something big in sewage.

Patsy Parkin had gone to America to work with the mentally disabled. Who'd have thought it?

Madge Badge had become a head teacher. Yes, a fitting end for a superior being.

Fat Bea had grown up slim and beautiful and married a dentist like her Dad.

Suze and I were friends for forty years, but finally realising that we had nothing but the past in common, we drifted amicably apart.

My Dad, sofa-Jack and Sean had all left me, and now Mark too and that was fine. I was whole and ready to begin my life from scratch. And being whole, I was able to look at the past, although I was afraid.

I drove back down the road, parked, walked tremulously up the path and knocked on the door of the house where I grew up.

An elderly couple stared at me from the doorstep while I

asked if I could come in, explaining that I had lived in the house as a child and would dearly love to see it again. They stood aside and I wandered around, looking in all the rooms, seeing snapshots of the past in my mind.

I was hoping to unlock more juicy traumas, some sensational material that I had perhaps forgotten because it was too awful. But I was disappointed. Instead of traumas and rows, I was surprised to see pictures of ordinary days flashing through my mind. I was shocked by the simple mundanity of it all. Was that what my childhood was really like?

The few traumas I had experienced were significant and cut deep, but there were many ordinary days and those were the days I had forgotten. For the whole of my life I had clung religiously to the pain, convinced that whatever happiness there was in my early years had only happened outside the house under green leaves and sunshine, whilst the inside was all misery and chaos.

It wasn't true.

I saw myself at six, jumping up and down with excitement on the dining room table with its green chenille cloth as the Beatles arrived home from their tour of America in 1964.

I saw Jane making up the coal fire in the living room and inadvertently setting fire to the carpet.

I saw myself again, watching *Doctor Who* from behind the sofa; and another time, curled up in the armchair with a chocolate éclair to watch The Avengers.

I saw Pussy run out the back door so fast she broke her

teeth on the coal bunker; and, on a different day, the budgie flying insanely around the room while we all shrieked and tried to get her back in the cage.

In the kitchen, I watched Chrissie's boyfriend Dan throw a ball of wool into my milk and Weetabix, and duck when I threw it back at him so it hit Mum soggily in the face. How we laughed at her surprise!

In that shabby little Sixties house I saw all these silly, happy, ordinary days.

I came home that night, confused and trying to process what I'd learned.

And while I was thinking, I remembered something else...

When I was little, I loved my Mum so much that I made her many drawings, all painstakingly coloured, of ballet-dancing ladies with pointy hands, with two fingers outstretched to make a line from shoulder to fingernail; or of medieval ladies with very tall witches hats with chiffon scarves that floated sublimely from their tips; and I gave them to her with love.

I realised that somewhere along the road from childhood to adulthood I'd started to blame my Mum for everything, not just the daft things she said to me but for all her mistakes; all hers and Dad's and mine too; for all my sorrow at my father's violence and abandonment; and for all the pain of watching her being abused by him.

I blamed my Mum entirely, when she was, after all, only doing the best she could. Now, finding myself in her moccasins, a single parent struggling to bring up teenage children on my own, I saw with clarity at last what I had done. And was she any more faulty and eccentric than I am?

270

I thought of this and cried, covering my eyes with my hands while the tears made holes in my hands and fell to the ground like acid rain, as I realised the deep truth about my life: that once I was a victim… and then I became a volunteer.

I did it to myself.

That was one of the gifts that came to me wrapped in cancer. And strange as it may sound I would not easily give up the gift of my cancer experience.

So what if I have scars and lumps and bumps? While I was fussing and fretting about the size and shape of my body, the menopause snuck up on me and laid all to waste anyway.

Now I wake up with a face that looks like it's been slept in all night. I have the beginnings of a moustache and wrinkles that reveal more character than I ever thought I had and certainly don't want.

But I have all that in common with my peers. For once, I am not the first. And I am looking forward to whatever lies ahead with the expectation of happiness, because I have looked the bogey-man straight in the eye and lived to tell the tale.

Few people are lucky enough to be able to say that.

ACKNOWLEDGEMENTS

THANKS:

To Mike Sharpe, my English teacher, for his encouragement. To Gerard Baker and Tim Rostron, who told me I could write. To Lloyd Davis, who persuaded me to share my diary, and had the idea to interweave the childhood and cancer anecdotes.

Special thanks to Katharine King who mentored me, Lucia White who was my sounding-board and Raymond Allen who always made me laugh. Also to Annie Ashdown, Jill Robinson and Phil Parker who got me back on course when I floundered.

My agents Isobel Dixon and Julian Friedmann for their patience and encouragement and my publisher Ben Yarde-Buller, editor Helen Zaltzman and publicist Fran Yarde-Buller.

The Dunford Novelists, who implored me to finish, especially Della Galton, Emma Nicholson, Michael Jones, Jill Butcher, Tess Kimber, Felicity Fair-Thompson, Caroline Praed, Jean Saunders, Marion Hough, Ena Richards, Jane Wenham-Jones, Dee Williams, Gordon Wells, Janet Jerram, Stuart Drinkwater, Pat O'Keefe, Jennifer Margrave, Gail Slater, Jean Sutton, Julia O'Sullivan, Martin Hall, Carole Westron, David Kendrick, Wendy Metcalfe, Annie Probin, Kim Hudson, Myra Kersner, Eileen Robertson, Susan Skinner, Echo Irving, Anne Ashurst and many more.

My test readers, whose feedback was invaluable: Alison Smith-Squire, Georgina Morley, Francesca Elston, Janice Kate Fisher, Shelagh Hamilton and Jean Moss.

To the people who helped and healed me at the time of my cancer, too many to thank, but here are some: Maureen Burge, Sheila Cotton, Jill Lenane, Brietta Pinder, Elaine Shaw, Chris Kershaw, Marion Howells, Chris Thompson, Liz Reid, Paul Green, Carol and Tony Madison, Lorraine Naested, Rex Bennett, Anne and Steven Jones, Amer & Judy Sarsaam, Wendy Hoy, Jane and Steve Barden, Caroline and Keith Chapman, Jacquie and Rob Glinyetski, Amanda and David Adkins, Cathy Page, Sarah and Paul Fielding, Annie and Mike Dixon.

The girlfriends who walked the journey with me, especially Geraldene Walsh, Jan Maddern, Helen Williams, Carol Walker, Angela Beattie and Sarah Dixon.

The dear friends who insisted on decorating my flat when I was in hospital, including Steve Ingham, Nigel Foster, Felicity Rock, Elaine Sutton, Paul Anthony, Max Wiseberg and Marion and John Hall-Hall.

The musician friends who played at benefit concerts for me, especially Martin Litton, Michael and Alan Bennett-Law, Keith Nicholls, Graham and Suzy Read, Martin Wheatley, Enrico Tomasso, Mike Henry, Joan Viskant, Stacey and Jim Kent, Mark Alloway, Randy Colville, Tony Davis, Richard and Joy Pite, Dave Green, Mike Piggot, Nils Solberg and Pete Morgan. To my Mum, my Dad, my sisters and my brother; Fat Bea, Madge Badge, Suze, Kathy Carter and Patsy Parkin.

And most of all my children, for putting up with their mum.

Janice Day is a patron of CANCERactive, the UK's largest cancer charity for evidence-based information on holistic cancer therapies. Started by Chris Woollams, a bio-chemist whose daughter's death inspired him to set up the charity, it is uniquely independent of pharmaceutical companies, vitamin providers, complementary therapies or alternative practitioners. The charity offers information on orthodox, complementary and alternative cancer therapies. Its mission is to enable people to build a perfectly tailored, integrated cancer therapy programme for their personal needs and their specific cancer, thus giving them the best possible chance of beating the disease.

CANCERactive.com.
Intelligent information. Independent voice.